PATRICE CHAPLIN
renowned playwright a
lished more than two ___. ᴜᴜᴜᴋꜱ. ʜer most
notable works include *Albany Park*, *Siesta* (which
was made into a film starring Jodi Foster and Isa-
bella Rossellini), *Into the Darkness Laughing*, *Hidden Star*, *Night
Fishing* and *Death Trap*. Her stage play *From the Balcony* was
commissioned by London's National Theatre in conjunction with
Radio 3. As a bohemian in Paris during the 50s and 60s, Patrice
spent time with Jean-Paul Sartre and Simone de Beauvoir. Married to Charlie Chaplin's son Michael and living and working in
Hollywood, she was associated with Lauren Bacall, Miles Davis,
Salvador Dali, Marlon Brando and Jean Cocteau, who gave her a
starring role in one of his films.

In her books *City of Secrets* (2007), *The Portal* (2010) and now *The
Stone Cradle*, Patrice opens the door to entirely new and compel-
ling elements of the Rennes-le-Château mystery involving the
mysterious Catalan capital of Girona.

Patrice is the director of The Bridge, a non-profit organization
that leads workshops based in the performing arts as a new and
unique way to help fight addiction. She resides in North London.

THE STONE CRADLE

ONE WOMAN'S SEARCH FOR THE
TRUTH BEYOND EVERYDAY REALITY

PATRICE CHAPLIN

CLAIRVIEW

Clairview Books Ltd.,
Russet, Sandy Lane,
West Hoathly,
W. Sussex RH19 4QQ

www.clairviewbooks.com

Published in Great Britain in 2017 by Clairview Books

All photos are taken from the author's private collection except colour plate of Girona by Internalfox at English Wikipedia

The right of Patrice Chaplin to be identified as the author of this work has been asserted in accordance with sections 77 and 78 of the Copyright, Designs and Patents Act, 1988

A CIP catalogue record for this book is available from the British Library

Print book ISBN 978 1 905570 83 6
Ebook ISBN 978 1 905570 84 3

Cover by Morgan Creative featuring ghostly figure © alswart;
old keyhole © Denis Rozhnovsky; rural street © Marc;
back cover image © Chris Chaplin
Typeset by DP Photosetting, Neath, West Glamorgan
Printed and bound by 4Edge Ltd, Essex

'Life is a gift from the few to the many, from those who know and have to those who do not know and have not.'

— Amadeo Modigliani

DRAMATIS PERSONAE

While the events and circumstances described in this book are true, the names of some places and most individuals have been changed to protect their identities.

Dr Arnau — Custodian academic
Beryl — Young London traveller in the late 50s
Jean Cocteau — Artist and film-maker
Filip Coppens — Writer
Salvador Dali — Artist
Lewis Doyle — Owner of TV and broadcasting studios in the US
Andrew Gough — US writer and magazine owner, explorer in metaphysical
Anna — Psychotherapist
Arve H — Man of enterprise
Holland — Teacher
Howard Hughes — US businessman
Peter Jack — TV producer
Cynthia le Kuche — Student and Model
Liliane — Guide on the journey of the Great Bear Constellation
Luis — Bar owner
Nachmanides — Renowned Cabalist and scholar of Girona
Ramon Masia — Catalan bookshop owner
Kathleen McGowan — Writer
Miguel — Restaurant manager
Gyp Planas — Effective military and police trained specialist in security
Kim — Lawyer
Otto Rahn — Grail writer
Sal Roca — Assistant to Salvador Dali
Abbe Saunière — Priest
Soham — Guru
José Tarres — Custodian
Maria Tourdes — the French woman, owner of the house with the tower
Ani Williams — Troubadour and writer

Foreword

When I first crossed the iron bridge into the ancient city of Girona in North East Spain I was 15 years old, and felt I had arrived in a place that was not of this world. It was too rich in atmosphere, the notes of its scale too high. It was magical. I still believe that today, although for different reasons. The people of Girona said then that the city has a mystery that pulls certain people back, time and again. A city's love never dies.

At first, I thought the mystery concerned the matching towers of Girona and Rennes-le-Château in France, creating a golden mean—a dynamic which, when activated, revealed a gap at its mid-point precisely at the peak of Mt Canigou. This is 'a portal', a gap in the planet's atmosphere leading to other places and other times. A private society has held this secret for centuries. Its power in the wrong hands would bring untold darkness. Many had sought the secret, including the Hapsburgs, Howard Hughes, Otto Rahn—the German Grail writer—and the enigmatic priest, Abbé Saunière from Rennes-le-Château. He made unexplained journeys to and from Girona at the end of the nineteenth century. I wrote about the society and the priest in *City of Secrets* and thought that the mystery was solved.

So, back there in the late 1950s I loved the city at first sight and also the man waiting at the end of the iron bridge: José Tarres, protector of his province from Franco and custodian of the private society, holder of the secret. After an illness in 2003, he gave me some of the material held by the society. He had hoped it would be made public when the world became a more optimistic place. I understood Girona was one of eleven sites on a transforming journey under the constellation of the Great Bear. I was given a guide who took me on the journey to the Portal on Mt Canigou and I understood that activity in that space, travelling through to

1

other realms, was the secret. For this, Howard Hughes and others had come to the area in the 1930s. I wrote *The Portal* and thought that the story was concluded.

Then came mention of the Stone, one of the oldest on the planet. There, in the centre of the journey under the constellation, was the secret so many had sought, and I understood finally that this might be why I was drawn, time and again, back to this place. And, why there was a hidden society, kept impeccable since antiquity, and what had happened before even this antiquity as we knew it. And it is of untold beauty, light and surprise. Once touched, you would always return, even in your dreams. Yet it has a certain danger. What is its purpose?

I have brought and taken much to and from this city. I was there at the uncovering of the Jewish Kabbalist Centre, glorious in the medieval ages but hidden since the expulsion in 1492. That, too, has many secrets. It was a great surprise for the locals of Girona. The meteor, further north, would be even more so...

Patrice Chaplin, January 2017

Prologue

There were three men waiting at the top of the narrowing eighth-century street where it squeezed itself around the buttress and away towards the cathedral. Was it the way the light fell that made their appearance unnerving? They were silent in the deserted siesta hour as I climbed the cobbled hill towards them and instinctively I tried to look younger and fitter as though to show I could take care of myself. It must be the way the sun lit their faces. They stood too straight, too tense, waiting. Nearer now, I could see their expressions were too hard for what was simply an introductory meeting. The words of my last US interviewer came to mind: 'Don't you feel frightened doing the stuff you do?' My walk was now untidy and I considered stopping and letting them come down the hill towards me. I assumed we were going to the L'Arc bar. Then I recognized Señor Masia from the second-hand bookshop. How could his expression be anything but friendly? And young, beautiful Roca whom I'd met only the day before seemed not to know me, yet he'd set up this meeting in the first place and we were already on good terms. The other, the powerful one I did not know, yet he was not unfamiliar.

The heat was tricky and the fact I'd been told there would be just one man, unnerving. A mere handshake, a greeting, the smiles were there now and then the powerful one embraced me, so putting me into the midst of the group and hugged amongst them I was walked swiftly up the street and to the right into a short, thin passage that I didn't recall seeing before. I'd been to and fro this ancient city since I was 15. What didn't I know about the old quarter? Obviously not enough.

Shadowed, private I judged the passage to be opposite Masia's bookshop. In a hurry now, they led me down through a low doorway into a darkened deep-vaulted stone room. There was no choice about it and their behaviour was swift and decided and I

3

was placed on a chair and the huge walls around came alive with light and sound. If I hadn't have known of this meeting I would have believed it had all the appearance of a kidnap. The powerful one took a seat behind a table in the gloom somewhere in front of me. Why hadn't I been introduced to him? His manner I thought was familiar. The hair was different, but I decided I had seen him briefly twice in different light and very different circumstances. I thought someone called him Gyp. Was this the apparent guardian of the city who no one could identify, who travelled seemingly unnoticed through the streets, a man José described as 'not without a certain danger'?

The walls, now visible, were covered with projected images, mostly photographs, circling slowly, some large as posters. They were all of me. And behind me figures slipped through the gloom drawing close, making no noise; grey nondescript people, all of them men. I could just see the powerful man's expression. It was beyond hate or love or anything I could identify. Sounds began, disquieting, turning ominous, too loud until it was not possible for me to hold this level of volume. The room was the work of an obsessive and all of it about me and my life. As the sounds increased photographs flicked on, switched off and were replaced by others more and evermore going into my past. Whoever had done this knew me inside and out: my wedding day, my children, the modelling days, the Hollywood years, my drama school productions, my bohemian days, the *Paris Match* spreads and José. My life came towards me on waves of sound, an attack, an intrusion. The man who might be Gyp sat between the brilliant walls and was covered in differing lights and pieces of my reflected life. All I was here for was a meeting about a project on ancient Girona where I would be offered 'an opportunity that would please me' — Roca's words of the previous day.

Where was he exactly? I looked behind me quite horrified by the increasing number of these shadowy men still arriving from all sides. No sign of Roca.

'Who are you?' I shouted at the one behind the desk. I thought he said, 'Your guardian.'

4

Smaller, grainy photos now, enlarged from snapshots, private, personal, going back through the early years and some I didn't know and wondered how they could have obtained these. I said this was terrible. Any sound was drowned by the noise and the chilled dark had filled up with 30 or 40 men, I was sure I did not know. The street door was closed.

Gyp leaned forward and claimed my attention. 'You look for the secret. Some of this you have. You've worked hard for your age,' he told me.

In spite of the position I seemed to be in I was still young enough to dislike that remark.

'But you cannot uncover more.'

It occurred to me then I could just get up and leave. Something about this man kept me attentive and still, as though this was the attitude he needed to obtain.

'We will give you the secret.' His voice was strong and rich as a preacher's and rose above the hellish noise. 'No one in this city has ever thanked you for the work you have done. Many don't even know you. You are unsung. But we will show our gratitude. You will be offered something that will please you because you deserve it.' His voice and the sound from the walls jarred unacceptably, and I covered my ears. I was in something that was beyond acceptable even for me. I was the object of ritual, a sacrifice, perhaps revenge. It occurred to me most succinctly that I could be slaughtered. And the photographs pushed their way into my consciousness, my whole life a punishment, the sounds arranged in hypnotic order to break me down.

'You will be offered the role necessary to be shown the secret. And then you will be initiated and remain here in this city.' His voice was too deep finding its way through the discordant noise.

'No!' And I curled forward in the chair, hands still over my ears, eyes shut tight, feet clattering on the stone, closing off the unbearable.

'Come and see what we offer you.' He rose from his chair. 'All is yours. Just climb the stairs with us.'

Never. That was where they would do it. And it would look like

5

an accident. He opened his arms generously. 'All this is for you: the house, the gardens, the land. Your expenses paid ... everything. You are the chosen one, the next in the custodial line and the last. You are the last. You have the secret.'

He'd said it all. I think he waited for me to be grateful.

My legs were shaking and I hoped my heart would be on my side and stand up to what came next. Its beating was the flutter of a trapped bird.

And the men crowded closer, not quite flesh and blood, wrapped in the grey mist. And I had the one last thought that might save me.

'José. What does he say about this?'

'José Tarres.' Gyp gestured with his hands, a full satisfying indication of doom. 'He is finished.'

He was coming towards me and I wished I had some of that 'not bad for my age strength' he'd mentioned. I'd give him one in the place that hurt.

'Be wise now and follow what is offered.'

He was close, but didn't touch me. Could I just run around the men to the heavy door and into the unknown street, which had been surely uncovered for this private occasion, as if by medieval ritual? I could see the mention of José would buy me nothing in here. God would be a better ally.

'What's the matter with her?' asked the man behind me.

'She hasn't come round to it yet.' Gyp was impatient. 'She still thinks she has a choice.' He looked at me. 'You are the most disobedient.'

And the years I'd passed through, with a fair share of pain and adversity, were surely good for something. I straightened up and looked at this rich-voiced captor.

'José won't like this. You'll have to answer to him. And we'll see who has choice. He won't forgive you for this.'

And I wasn't sure of my territory as far as José was concerned, of what, if anything, he would do to save or avenge me. And my body started to swirl around with the many versions of me around the walls and my heartbeat was lost in the threatening drumming

6

from the stone room and my life, in all its complexities, seemed very short.

He still held out his hand to help me from the chair. The photographs were circling madly like a fairground ride gone wrong and the sounds stuck in an atonal chord. I thought I said, 'My money's on José.'

'He's gone. We've put him on a train for Paris.' Dismissive, then, of José. 'You won't win,' I promised.

He tried again to take my hand, to lead me away. 'I think you should see what I offer you.'

The men waited, a little restless now. Was their leader going to let them down? 'The trouble is, you will stay now. No choice there.' His voice was quiet, just for him and me. The atonal stuck sound fading, images running into each other, upturned, rolling down from all my past like a multiple road accident.

'Stay? Oh, I don't think so.'

He looked almost surprised.

'I'll go away.' And I straightened up, ready to leave.

'Away?' he echoed. 'Where?' He was definitely surprised. 'How?'

'I'll just go.' And it was almost time for me to get up from the chair.

'But there's nowhere to go.' He paused, almost sad. 'You're in it and it's in you.'

And I thought, I know this man Gyp. And in that moment I knew I would never be free.

1

I first heard of the Portal when I was 15 and hitchhiking through France with my friend, Beryl. We were travelling, taking the roads as they came not running away but forwards towards a freedom which was undeniably ours. Out of the London suburbs into an intriguing way of life unknown but not altogether unfamiliar. This was the mid-50s and there was still an innocence about that time which allowed us this way of travel not possible in later years. We were bohemians to the core, dressed in the obligatory style of the outsider, the kind that frequented the Trad Jazz clubs of Soho, a style taken up by poets, painters and individuals called 'characters': black drainpipe trousers, fisherman's sweater duffel coat from Charing Cross Road, rope sandals, ankle chains with bells, hoop earrings, big kiss curls, white lipstick, black nail polish.

However bizarre, it couldn't hide Beryl's beauty which on occasion made being her friend quite difficult. We danced Rock and Roll, Boogie, Jive, Trad Jazz. We had a joy of life.

We crossed the French border into Spain and were stopped by the frontier police. They had never seen anyone like us and admitted it. No one looked like us. What were we? Extraterrestrials?

'They've come through the Portal,' the men decided, trying to laugh.

It sounded good and we asked if the Portal was a club that we'd somehow missed on the journey south. A policeman pointed to the nearby mountain, its peak visible on this bright day. He said the Portal was right there on the summit.

'It leads from here to other places, so they say.'

How had we passed through France they wanted to know?

'The nervous French would kill you and cook you.' More laughter.

They still held our passports and papers. You had to have a visa to get into Spain in those days and ours seemed in order. The young policeman pointed at Beryl's rope sandals. 'You come from Roman times?' He dared to check her duffel coat, one quick exploratory touch, just to make sure. It was just the usual earthly fabric. I could begin now to understand my father and the effect our style of dress had on him and why he so readily arranged our special youth passports giving the reason 'to further the girls' education'. He obviously couldn't take the assault of our appearance on his necessary conformity in that uptight suburb between London and the countryside. I told him to add 'learning French for future secretarial position'. He was glad to blot that ink dry.

The cops still held our visas and passports and were unsure about our age, legitimate right to be travelling, money, status and the driver of the car who had picked us up in Toulouse. This jolly, friendly man who had sung French songs throughout the hot afternoon had become decidedly edgy. It seemed he didn't appreciate the delay.

The official in charge asked what we were and we answered honestly. 'Gypsies.' We might head to where the flamenco singers lived in Seville. He asked why we weren't at school. Because we were travelling into the unknown. If it wasn't for our appearance they would have stopped us as runaways. But we were too odd for even that. In Paris we'd spend nights at Sidney Bechet's club and mornings with Jean-Paul Sartre and Simone de Beauvoir and they had given us new identities. We were existentialists they said, we didn't cling to the past or fear the future. We lived only in the moment. That sounded about right and nothing much would have changed that description if the unthinkable hadn't happened: I fell in love and life as it had given me freedom took it back and I was grounded.

Beryl — her language was better than mine — got the policemen off mundane matters of age and birth and asked about the Portal.

'It leads to places not normally understood. The inhabitants aren't from round here.'

She liked that. 'So, you go from here to there?'

'And you don't come back, they say.'

Beryl said we should check it out one of these days and the official at last stamped our passports and gave back the visas and we were ready to go and then all hell broke out. A border guard had opened up our driver's car and it was discovered he was smuggling arms into Spain using us as cover. Shots were fired and Beryl and I ran for it and hours later ended our journey by horse and cart into the pre- Roman city of Girona in NE Spain, just across the Pyrenees mountain range.

Years later I wrote about that arrival in my book *Albany Park*. The sky was violet and flashing with huge flat stars. The sun was setting behind the last bridge in a blaze of scarlet rage. The narrow streets were filled with music, heady perfume, the smell of woodsmoke. The church bells chimed as though for a celebration and then all the lights of the city came on, hundreds of yellow eyes. It was a true welcome. I knew that if I crossed the clanking iron bridge built by Eiffel and stepped onto the other bank I'd be in an unimaginable land, changed forever. Radio stations in the apartments and bars played a haunting Spanish song, I assumed was a chartbuster. It was in fact an advertising jingle for chocolate. The music was full of the melancholy desire that Spain conjured up and I thought it announced the beginning of a huge even deadly passion. How right I was.

I crossed the bridge and at the other side awaited José Tarres. Charismatic poet, defender of the Catalan province against the rape of Franco's dictatorship he helped other activists to safety across the mountains into France. Keeper of the old customs that had survived centuries he celebrated his birthplace with the traditional fiestas, dances and rituals, kept going the forbidden Catalan language, making the city come alive and unlike any other. He was unlike anyone I had ever met and over the years that didn't change. I knew him completely and utterly from the first glance and felt that the whole of my short life until then had been merely a time of waiting. From bohemian I became novia (fiancée) and I stayed with him in paradise. For a while.

The Girona Bridge, designed by Eiffel, crosses from the new part of Girona into the mysterious old quarter

Hollywood at the end of the 60s was a good time and I had two of my published books under option to a studio and an independent producer was interested in an idea on Girona. I was recording a documentary for the BBC on the *British in Hollywood*. Married with two children I lived in Kentish Town NW London and I was going back for a play to be later produced at the National Theatre. I was about to have lunch at Ma Maison with my superstar idol of all time. I was at the top of my game. And to my amazement I felt empty. And then someone mentioned a Portal and described an invisible channel into space and I was back in the 50s at the Spanish frontier with Beryl and the Portal story. And then I thought of José. And that's when I knew why I had felt such emptiness. He was the one to open the champagne with. It felt as though I was running physically to LA airport. The plane journey to Barcelona was long but not long enough to sort my past.

I arrived at the hotel in Girona where I had last seen José years ago and couldn't go in. I was scared to see him changed or with someone else. He could have slipped out of his exquisite skin and become ordinary. Also he may not be there. I hadn't seen or heard about him for five years.

The concierge came out of the dairy with a litre of Leche Ram milk and was pleased to see me. Cautiously I asked for José.

'But of course, he's here. Where else could he be? He can't leave Girona.' I should have taken more notice of that remark. And we climbed the well-remembered stairs together, the door of the salon opened and José stood against the wall, part of a dream and on the wall a big gold tin sun decoration just behind his head like an aura. Then his eyes lit up and he came towards me with a soft tread and it was as though we had never been apart, the time in between did not exist. 'I knew you would come back,' he said.

I said he hadn't contacted me. How could he? I had never sent a message or address. 'Oh, but I reach you by thought.' His eyes as they stayed on mine promised everything was still in place. 'Let's go to the Arc bar. Luis will be so happy to see you.' And we walked out into the evening as we had innumerable times in the past. There were lots of friends from the old days in the bar that night but I only really saw José.

On the third day I knew I should be back in LA or lose my writing deal with the producer. His tone when I had called that day from the hotel had made it clear. How did I tell José I had to leave? We still talked of the future we were meant to share. It was agreed we belonged together, the link was too strong. I said I had to go back to the film in LA and then on impulse I asked him to come with me. He did hesitate. Then he said he needed to restore a courtyard in the old quarter. And there was something about a gallery and a flower show. He could not leave. I had to leave. But what was between us couldn't leave either. I believed that would never change.

Good things happened in the next years and I had my share of celebration but the top note of high happiness was missing. Yes, he was the one to open the champagne with. I wrote about our early years together both in *Albany Park*, then *Siesta* which was later filmed with music by Miles Davis. When the reality of Girona became memory, it seemed even more vibrant. Perhaps that was how legends were born. José had always been out of reach, except perhaps in those moments when he appeared suddenly in my thoughts. A sense of him would suddenly come to me in a rain-soaked summer street, the smell of woodsmoke would bring him instantly and then I knew that I'd have to go back there. On one occasion finally I hurried to my house in Kentish Town and they, the children and my husband, looked up pleased I was there. How could I say I was going? I felt I was an intruder in their innocence, worse, a murderer of their reality. They were so calm and trusting. All was as it should be in this sweet room. My husband I would never hurt. I prayed for God to take away this passion I could not deal with and lift it out of my heart and keep it in his care.

My husband, Michael Chaplin. Unique, an old soul — we had some memorable times

The following year I went to Spain on a short business project with my publisher nowhere near Girona and on the way back to the airport a stone stuck in a wheel of the taxi.

The driver had to stop in a deserted village and change the tyre. I crossed into the shade of a side street. Just one man, leaning against a wall. Our eyes met.

Marriage over. He did say when I first met him that you can't lose what truly belongs to you even though you throw it away.

José came to London — something to do with an artefact. It had mistakenly been put up for auction and he had to get it back. It sounded like a metaphor for our dilemma. I couldn't leave my husband. It took months of indecision and pain and it was the hardest thing I ever did.

Spring 1969 I lived with José in a fisherman's house on the Catalan coast with the children. One night we drove up into the hills and watched all the lights come on in Girona: a cluster of colour, a superb necklace, resplendent with gems. As if some unaccepted lover had adorned the nakedness of the city celebrating its power. 'Of course, there are those who leave gifts here. And secrets. It is the right place for those. Always has been. No one owns Girona,' he said.

I too would have to make an offering in the end. I'd not get away untouched. And then he said, 'Something always comes in the way of what I want.' Uneasy now I said he didn't have to make a secret of whatever it was.

'You mentioned secrets,' he said. 'There is an old society in Girona that takes care of those. And I have to take over the society.'

'Why you?' I knew now, there'd be no living together in a place of peace that he'd promised away from the calls on his time. All that was rosy-future talk.

Remembering his activist past I supposed it was related to that.

'Because I am the right person. It is what I have been prepared for all my life.'

I asked if it was the Freemasons and he said something like that. I asked what this meant for us. He said we would stay as we were and nothing would come in the way of that.

For some days we lived harmoniously in the village and then between one hour and the next anxiety started. He blamed it on the Tramuntana, the mountain wind and then I saw the car with the foreign number plates and the driver just sitting in the front, watching the sea.

'He's from my husband and the family,' I said.

And the man came to the door and the deal was clear: if I did not go back to the UK I lost the children. It came down to survival. I would never lose my children. I went back to London to divorce.

Girona was the place for secrets. I'd heard mention of an archaic society. It protected a secret from the beginning of time. In existence for centuries the society was made up of professional men of standing and an initiate group which performed rituals and affected change to enable the hidden to be experienced. Some said it was akin to alchemy and the calling up of spirits. The nucleus of this secret was arrived at by following a journey through eleven sites under the constellation of the Great Bear and the sites were linked and matched using sacred geometry and presented a mirrored landscape and on this Girona and Rennes-le-Château, a village just over the border in France, were connected. I gathered this information from whispers across the years.

Another secret concerned the impoverished priest, Bérenger Saunière of Rennes-le-Château who in the 1890s between a day and a night became phenomenally rich and I understood he had made discrete journeys to the house with the tower behind the Girona Cathedral to visit a young French woman, Maria Tourdes, who had installed herself there in 1891. In those days it was unthinkable for a woman, and more an outsider, to live un-cha-peroned in this conservative Spanish city. It was recorded that to activate the dynamic of the mirrored landscape Saunière had copied her tower in 1904 for his parish. It was said he was in the pay of the Hapsburgs and in fact had bought the Girona property in which he'd placed Maria Tourdes so he could make visits, always after dark, entering discreetly by the city wall. After his death in 1917 she married a much older man and continued living in the house until the middle of the 1960s when she left for Paris.

I remember going to her garden in the 1950s and swinging from the royal palm tree. She had a sardonic style, understood my love for the city and the man and gave wise advice. She was the first sophisticated woman I'd met and she liked silk stockings and Houbigant and Worth perfumes. Was it she who had mentioned Kabbalistic magic and the Jews of Girona? That subject had certainly been kept secret. Shortly after Maria Tourdes left Girona, the house with the tower was pulled down and between one night and one day it had gone. Only a few broken walls were left standing, abandoned. Even the royal palm tree was hacked up, its huge root lying there as though wounded, gaping to the sky. And

I asked who was responsible and José said, 'The one who wants what is hidden there but it's too late. Poor thieves in the night. The treasure is already gone long ago.' And later he mentioned 'El Americano' whose men had taken everything apart stone by stone looking for the secret the historic society held.

It was said that the stones of Girona had a magnetism that drew certain people back time and again. I was told it had to do with ley lines and at certain points across the earth the energy builds and creates a pull, a pulse and in those places unusual things happened.

The spirit of Girona was what mattered. It had to approve of you otherwise you passed through that old quarter and it would show you nothing. I believe that the spirit of the city approved of me, as I was then. Of course it would not let me go. A city's love did not die.

Girona had been an Iberian trading centre dating from 3000 years BC and the Phoenicians landed on the coast and then the Greeks in 2000 BC. The Romans left their mark, building much of what is the old quarter and Charlemagne marched into the city, left his influence as did Napoleon III. Girona won the Moorish contest but lost centuries later to Franco in the 1930s Civil War. Every invader left his imprint. Situated between the frontier with France and Barcelona to the south Girona had always been a city of passage. Anonymous travellers passing through left little trace making it a good place to hide what must never show its name. Over the years I did write about that enchanted time. I wrote film scripts, documentaries and my work was occasionally translated into Catalan and Spanish. My second stage play performed in Paris was staged at the Girona festival, a prestigious event held every autumn.

When I saw José again I'd remarried and he was now involved in trying to restore the unknown Jewish quarter which had been closed off since the expulsion in 1492. The Jewish presence was considered the Golden Age of Girona, the home of medieval scholars and mystics, the centre of Kabbalah. For the modern inhabitants this centre of Kabbalah was a big surprise. José's

16

money had run out and I wrote articles for Jewish papers, the *LA Times*, and produced a documentary for the BBC. It brought in enough funding just to keep it going. If it could have done the same for us.

The truth was we were changed people. I was no longer the travelling girl crossing the iron bridge ready for any experience, full of life, love and he wasn't the divine poet who brightened lives and would give his own to free his town.

José was 42 and there was nothing to fight any more and people wanted to forget Franco and that dark time and in some ways he was out of date. He had no wife, no child and said he could not leave Girona. His obligations were to the place and I assumed he was still custodian of the society.

He occasionally saw a future for us: we would live on the coast, I would have his child, my children would go to Spanish schools, our lives would be simple, replete. Everything was still in his rosy future and stopped me paying attention to the present which had all the answers already there, only too clear. He would never leave the city he loved more than any woman.

Having left my first husband for José I would not lose the second. The leaving for him had deprived my children of their father. I would not take them away from their school, neighbourhood friends, their security, or from my new husband who cared for them. I needed to write and the deals happened not in Girona but out there in the big world. That was where it worked for me. We hadn't managed to live our dream. The trouble was when I was away from José I remembered him as he had once been and that memory would not let go. He had been a gift from God.

He met the girl who gave him the baby, devotion, all he seemed to want, and she didn't leave for distant places and need other stimulus. He came back to me in my dreams and appeared against vividly coloured landscapes that I had never seen. I'd hear a woman say, 'The Portal, he comes from there.'

2

When José thought he was dying in 2003, he chucked me the secret of Girona like a hot potato and told me to write the book. He lived. I discovered he had given me only a part and asked for the rest.

'That you have to do yourself.' And the drawbridge went up and he would say no more. The research took months of climbing up hot, cobbled streets on often fruitless journeys. Increasingly, I became aware of the presence of the society and had a sense that change was happening. Some members feared that when José was no longer there the group would disband, go underground, and the material would be lost forever. These individuals gave me clues and evidence, the stuff of alchemic transformation. The core of the group was conservative and wanted the material to be sent to the Vatican. Some members did wonder what José had told me and sent, at least, two security agents on my track. *City of Secrets* was published in several countries and came out in Spain in 2007. It revealed an ecclesiastical cover up, the ghostly appearance of a lady carrying a cup, which had been witnessed over the centuries but could not be recorded or approved by the church. I also revealed the private society's existence which held the secret that could not see the light of day. The book mentioned the rituals and the initiates who performed them in the seminary in the Pyrenees. Dali and Jean Cocteau had both been society members. The masons in the Girona Scottish Rite 33 Degree had always a strong presence in the steering group. The Knights Templar had secreted treasure in Girona's Valley of San Daniel. What was the secret sought by so many in the past including the Hapsburgs, Otto Rahn, Hitler, Charlemagne, Arabs, Phoenicians, and the legendary El Americano? The society, tighter than Fort Knox, held it here in the city, unsuspected by local inhabitants. Was it similar to the practices the Jewish scholars and mystics carried out in medieval times taking them beyond the dimension of accepted reality, challenging the laws of the universe as we know it? Had they been privy to these secrets which emboldened their experiments? Here in the golden age of Kabbalah, Nachmanides, the renowned rabbinic scholar, wrote the formidable work, *The Book of Splendour*. Four Kabbalists made their historic journey into other realms, from which only one returned unharmed. It had been said the secret was better kept a secret than in the wrong hands. There was new information that the priest of Rennes-le-Château had sought this material which was defined as the Grail. He had copied the tower from the French woman's garden. Both towers were activated, creating a golden mean, opening the centre point on the peak of Mount Canigou. I was reminded of the frontier policeman's comments all those years ago, 'up there is the Portal. It leads to places people don't usually visit.' And there were references in the various correspondences from 1890 that the mountain peak held an opening that some said was the centre of the universe. It was, in later documents, named the Portal. Dali had experienced its effect on Perpignan station when he fell into another dimension. So the Portal it seemed was now the key point of the mystery. But how was it activated? How did a traveller go from that point and to where? I hadn't realized that what I unfolded was against church doctrine and I was advised to stop any research and all Portal claims.

City of Secrets made its mark in Girona and I was given an award the following April on St George's Day, the day of the book and the rose. The locals said it takes a stranger to tell us our own story. But I was no stranger.

So the Portal was the secret the archaic society had held for centuries. The local hotel owner, Señor Mons, told me the Portal was reached by a journey laid out under the constellation of the Great Bear, and that it wasn't exactly a tourist excursion. He added that people who came back from it were changed by the experience. I asked if it was religious.

'Not to do with the church. You can be sure of that.'

'Black magic?' I asked.

He didn't think the kind of people who were involved would be associated with magic. When he spoke of the ones who came back, I asked what happened to the others. His answer was not satisfactory. He introduced a few ironic Catalan jokes to get my mind off what he thought it should not be on anyway.

It was said José set up the guide, Liliane, who took me to the Portal. She was Hungarian and had given guidance to initiates on and off for some years. I did not know, at that time, she was a Hapsburg and had a successful worldly past. She made it clear the Portal could only be located and entered by those who had taken their journey of initiation. It took some weeks for me to tread with her the preparatory path through the eleven sites of Catalonia under the Ursa Mayor or Great Bear and reach the summit of Canigou.

I learnt that a Portal occurs at rare points where the earth atmosphere is thin and coincides with ley lines and energies, meeting and building a significant force. It is an invisible gap often referred to as a gateway, through which matter and spirit can leave and also re-enter our existence. The phenomenon allows contact with levels of reality beyond us and not normally within our reach. This contact can reclaim the past, existing on other levels and can facilitate and allow the re-entry of other entities, beings, knowledge to our planet. The calling up of material from the Portal has always been in the care of initiated individuals and in unwise hands the power of this process could, as I have been told, shed the planet into unthinkable darkness.

A Portal could only be activated by resonance from those who have built up the practice along the eleven sites and could attune with this barely existing gap. To enter a Portal was to be sucked into transformation and students, such as I, could effect changes in the self whereas chosen adepts effected changes on a global level and by their attunement put to rights much of this planetary darkness. The practice had been in existence since antiquity and Kabbalists in the Middle Ages have taken this Catalan path to aid God perfecting the universe.

I had no idea when I started the Portal journey in spring 2006 what it would demand. Liliane, the guide, dealt only with the present, refused all questions regarding the future. The past was a learning experience that could be healed and so to some extent, changed. I was allowed to read small passages from the accounts of those before me, including Jacint Verdaguer, the Catalan priest and poet. At once, I failed on the physical stuff and my body let me down immediately. Deprived of its comfort, it became weak and faint and how chuffed she was at that. I had done the unthinkable, spent a night alone in isolated country without running water, bottled water, a lavatory or light. I had shuddered at the creaking twigs heralding the possible footfall of an intruder wishing me harm, been bitten by every type of insect in the vicinity, and looked into the eyes of a rat. My fears, and I discovered they were my own and necessary, in my view, for the business of survival, were swatted like stubborn pests by this woman half laughing and incredulous that I could be made of such weak material.

I discovered what I thought I was, who I thought I had been, was an assertion that made her laugh aloud. That little ego would be stripped within the hour. The journey was a dive off a high board. I had been stretched beyond my modest limit, faced with possible death on two occasions. Lying in my own grave which she had helped me dig, shed much of an illusory past. I had been introduced to sacred numbers, symbols, and the underlying primal language beneath the everyday exchange we used. I had been encouraged to think out of the box and it had been rough. In spite of unbearable ambivalence, I had passed through my fears and into the Portal experience that gave a fairground ride to other places, other times, oddly not unfamiliar and afterwards I did feel a certain freedom. Fairground ride was the best way to describe the whirling, circling and suddenly stopping journey I had been privileged to experience, one without any control or input from me. She had laughed at the idea. 'Control? Faith would be a better ally.'

I did all right on one thing. Sometimes I could attune my mental energy and see the unseen. On occasion I had been described as mediumistic. I could on other occasions reach back into past times. That was what mattered. I could 'see' for them. Them?

The society, of course. That one quality made me valuable. Wasn't it their idea I do the journey? They just said it came from José. That's what Liliane said. You could not go further than a Portal. Surely nothing came after such an earthly challenge. How many things could I be wrong about? Too many.

Back in London, in 2006, I sat in my agent's office and shared an idea. 'You want to write about a Portal?' he said.

I tried to describe it but my agent would not let me finish. 'Will it sell at the checkout at Tesco?' This was his new criteria. He assured me publishing had changed, recession was rampant and the market seemed to rest on self-help sold at supermarket checkouts. He asked if the Portal was an object. I said it was metaphysical.

'Put the Grail on my office desk and you've got Tesco.' And he suggested sums no writer could believe. Of course, he meant the Grail, the Golden Cup they were all looking for, that would make Aladdin a has-been.

I still went ahead with the Portal book and a new set of enemies appeared. The Rennes-le-Château devotees claimed the mystery as theirs. What did Girona have to do with it?

Nicole Dawe, involved in restoring the French site, said how brave I was to publish on that subject at all, and she admired my courage. Why? I had no idea. I did later. But by then I had enough enemies on my hands in Girona. The Spanish publisher said the Rennes-le-Château crowd worried they would lose a few tourists and tea shop sales, but the Catalans were not after that kind of fame. I confirmed Girona had never sought attention but the opposite. I had been fortunate in the story to be at the place and time in the 50s when those pivotal people like Dali and Cocteau were around the French woman and her house in Girona.

When *City of Secrets* was published in the US there was quite a controversial response. I was contacted by NASA and asked if I would be willing to talk to a senior person in the establishment.

Another call and the senior official was put on the line. He had an attractive, educated voice that could be reassuring. Had I, in my experience with Portals, come across any artificial ones? I had never heard of that possibility. He explained that before NASA was founded, the space programme was run by the Government Aviation and in the 40s an American aviator had discovered a Portal and conducted research into the concept and created his own. He had not added one precaution: quarantine. Did I know the construct of a Portal? I did not. He emphasized energy and matter from this planet could go out through the gaps in the atmosphere and other matter could come in. Hence the need for quarantine. But the aviator wanted everything done quickly and a mishap occurred. I took that to mean a disaster. 'So we are attempting to destroy all artificial Portals.' Had I heard of the Black Box? I had not. Or the approach from a being thousands of light years out in space? A Portal without the quarantine filter had allowed an object to come through to our planet. When deciphered, it showed a being that would in 50,000 light years arrive on earth and it wanted us to know what it would look like. Was this the disaster? Turned out not.

He asked, if I should come across any artificial Portals, to let him know.

'But I only came across one in the Pyrenees. Where did this aviator find a Portal to copy?'

'In the Pyrenees.'

I should have asked about that. There were so many questions I should have asked, so many answers I would need to know. Why did I not ask who the aviator was? I assumed I wouldn't know the name. Would it mean anything to me or Girona? It would.

My agent couldn't laugh enough. 'NASA? And you believe it? Of course, it was —'

What word could he use but lunatic. The trouble was I didn't not believe it. I had never dealt with these matters in my life. What was the mystery? They all asked that. The unimaginable link between here and elsewhere that would give untold power to the user. Located on Mount Canigou, it could be activated by the two towers which Saunière and the Hapsburgs suspected. Yes, I had found a secret hidden for centuries. Of course, it was the Portal. What else?

It wasn't about that at all.

The Portal was published in 2009 by Quest and a few prestigious offers came forward for *The Portal* film rights but as my agent said they did not have follow through. The option went to a TV writer, Peter Jack, who took *City of Secrets*. My agent said he was keen and would get it made. I realized later why listening to his advice kept me a pauper. The PR girl, Xochi at the US publisher Quest had a sound knowledge of metaphysical subjects and started guiding me on who to trust and what to read. So she became both friend and adviser. I did presentations in bookshops and for the Theosophical Society. *The Portal* did all right but it did not make Tesco. Lewis Doyle, the self-styled voice of the metaphysical interviewed me for his New York outlets. He said I had pretty big stuff going if NASA was asking questions and that NASA would add credibility to my story. Why did I need it? Was I that unworldly? 'Every Grail-seeker, believer in the cults of Jesus and Magdalene will try and bring you down,' Doyle said. 'Because you have taken over their priest and you have got new material. You are a pioneer and you have changed the story.'

3

I first saw Gyp Planas in the Antigua, one of the oldest cafes in
Girona on a spring day when the rain was falling relentlessly, a
continuous curtain seemingly impenetrable through which
figures could be seen hurtling from one doorway to another, from
arcade to flooding alley. None of it offered the least hope of shelter
and the cobbled streets were ankle deep with rushing water.
Where the water was going was anyone's guess. Figures, inhuman
as dummies, lurching sideways, through this deluge which had
gone on unchanging since dawn. Umbrellas were all done with,
out of fashion they lay broken in the gutters. Peter Jack, puffed up
like a bird about to take flight, was here to try and get background
for the film script. The rain had drenched his hair in a way that
made it stand up straight in blades, a style a man like him would
not have dreamt of sporting even in his youth. His thin cheeks
reddening in the fug, eyes dripping, everything in his face cold
with shock or heated drastically, sweat waited across his forehead
to drip or freeze. He was maddened by the extremes of weather
and atmosphere. The customers at the iron tables, unchanged in
style since 1907, shouted weather bulletins into mobile phones or
roared with a laughter, which was mostly hysteria. Crockery
crashed, glasses spilt. The cafe was steaming up from the moist
fabric of dozens of drying coats. Shoes sodden out of shape lay
abandoned under the tables.

'It has never been like this.' The waitress handed out paper
towels and tried to mop the floor.

Peter Jack, with the English copy of *City of Secrets* in front of him
on the table, a pad and new pens to make notes, was holding tight,
perilously near to a panic attack. He rose up further in the chair.
'I'll get some air.'

'Air? Where from?'

The sheer volume of rain put him back at the table. This, his first visit to Girona was nothing like the book. 'José won't come,' he said. 'He won't get through this.' Panic now joining the general sense of possible catastrophe. Screech of a rescue vehicle. Peter Jack shivered and the sweat travelled down his face. He may never see his wife and children. Water moved silently under the door towards our table. I offered him a brandy and he tried to look reluctant. He was full of last thoughts and drank it in one go.

And then the door opened and one man came in. He was calm, he was utterly and always individual. No matter how many he was with, there always seemed to be a space around him so he was noticeable and alone. Some called it charisma. Ageless and exquisite, his hair a white cloud around his face, he moved through the cafe madness as though giving benediction, a greeting here, a handshake there, he certainly calmed them down.

Peter Jack, for a moment, forgot the climate. José wore a long brown coat and if it was wet, it wasn't noticeable. He had arrived from whatever point of departure and he was fine. So it was raining. It made no blot on his day. He smiled and his eyes brightened and then he really looked at me and time had no place here and again it was as though we had never been apart. He took off his coat and the waitress rushed to hang it for him. He touched my face just once, in greeting.

Yes, there was someone behind him. The man dealt with the rain by shaking himself briefly like a dog. It seemed they were together and we were now four around the table. The new friend had strength, agility and power and came out of things well. He would look after himself and possibly those around. José mentioned his name, which I immediately forgot. I did not know him. He wore a three-piece dark-green suit. No, I'd never seen him before and couldn't think what he was doing at this meeting. He sat beside me, and José took the chair opposite, next to Peter Jack, and I asked what they wanted to drink but the new friend took care of that at least for José and himself. Peter Jack and I were irrelevant to this stranger. He was just there, a witness at the table.

Peter Jack, preparing the film, was here in the cafe to meet the star of the book and wanted to be sure José was clear about the

26

film and the use of some of his past and his property. The first of the eleven sites was the country hut, the Barraca and its land. The next, the French woman's garden, was also in his care. José did not speak English, Peter Jack was okay in French. For a moment I wondered if the man in the three-piece suit (from then on he was '3 Piece'), was the interpreter but it seemed he knew no English. Throughout the conversation he sat next to me, solid, without speaking and didn't once look my way. I realized he wasn't big as much as powerful. I could feel it without looking at him. When he made a simple movement — he at one moment crossed his hands, it was as though something significant had happened. He got up and bought a cognac for José. I decided he was a bodyguard. He took care of things and I got the feeling he did not approve of either Peter Jack or me.

José defined what we could use. We could not enter the Barraca or the land, it was a divine site. Since when? I had entered it all my life. He would allow no groups or film crews in his garden. It was a private place, one of respect.

Peter Jack was taken aback. 'So, how do we film it?'

'From the distance.'

José looked at his companion. The meeting was not in my favour. For something to do I put my hand in my bag and took out the first thing I touched. It was a postcard repro of Dali's *Perpignan Station* — the 'portal' and I laid it on the table.

Was it to stress I was part of this business and deserved respect and to remind them I had known the artist? Was that why I placed the postcard in front of them? José barely looked at it and 3 Piece turned it around and spoke softly in Catalan. I thought he said, 'Oh, she shows us this.' He flipped it back. Yes, good with the hands. Peter Jack couldn't take his eyes off him. We were both subordinates and not doing well. I felt I should lift the profile a little and mention money. Neither took any notice. Then the waitress came to us with a camera and 3 Piece indicated where we should sit. This was unexpected and had never happened at Café Antigua. Obviously this man was a heavyweight in all ways and they wanted his photograph. A politician? 3 Piece asked for the

27

chairs to be placed in a line against the wall and we sat obediently and smiled.

Back around the table and one last shot. Satisfied he stood up and put a hand on José's shoulder. The cafe door opened and shut as more customers crowded in for shelter. A cinder-black-haired woman, half covered with a shawl, approached our table. She had a strength and bearing that was wearing a little thin with age and probable poor health. Something had driven her through the rain into this cafe and she would expect to get what she came for. I had never seen a face as hard, not the expression but the content. Her face was stone. Peter Jack turned, not quite believing what he was seeing. The face lacked too much, that was what disturbed him. The flesh was pulled tight and yellow-white and completely smooth with dark, dry eyes still and pitted with black points. There was a nose, a mouth, a chin, not relating to each other. Then the stone face turned to 3 Piece and she gestured to him to follow and in spite of the rain he left the cafe with her. It seemed she had come to get him.

'It must be the light,' said Peter Jack dealing with another shaky moment in a shaky day. 'Is she a member of the society? What about him?'

I did not know. The face was a stone. That was it.

I was more concerned with José. Would he stay? Would I see him again? All the earlier restrictions about the Barraca and land was more about our relationship than any film. Peter Jack did better in French now that 3 Piece was gone and said he was surprised and gratified José had got through torrential conditions to meet us. I said I didn't know of the earthly limits that stopped José if he really wanted something and Peter Jack saw another motive for the meeting. 'Oh, I get the subtext. So this is not entirely cinematic.' He laughed to show us, though it was his trip, it was all right with him. He opened his arms in deference to my love. José laughed. We were all laughing. I was screaming inside.

'She belongs to cinema, whatever she does,' said José carefully making it safe. 'There is no one like her. She creates it out of nothing.' Screaming? Howling! He was going to leave. This was the compliment before the farewell, the compliment I had come to dread. And then he suddenly lifted the mood and talked of Girona and the initiate's journey and brought an optimism and symmetry to the telling. The journey became worth fighting for and holding safe for those to come. It would bring light to our time and we certainly needed it. I could see Peter Jack was entranced. They would go on like this and José's allocation of unaccounted-for-hours in his marital negotiation would be used up. I asked Peter Jack to go for a walk, as I needed time alone. Walk? Was I so absorbed by José I had forgotten the world out there?

Puddles were now lakes. A sudden wind chucked rain at the windows. Peter Jack went instead to the bar and sampled the local wines from Perelada. I asked José the private things that could not wait another season. He said some of what I wanted to hear. It would always be just about one thing. We were born to be together and would never be together. As we talked it was as though it was just us alone at this iron table which became a makeshift craft taking us, two children of the deceiving past, across a lagoon of last hopes, still blue, still lapping smoothly. Linked like this? — impossible to let go. That had always been the joy and the problem. With a start he was drawn back into the cafe and he straightened up and saw a dozen creatures of gossip eyeing him.

He rose to go and I, now with him in this dreadful place, said the first thing that came to mind. I said Peter Jack was a good filmmaker. He did pause. 'That man will never make my film or tell my story.' I didn't like the sound of that.

The waitress got his coat. Peter Jack asked if he'd join us for dinner. 'I regret that I have to be somewhere else.' The somewhere was where the wife waited. I felt I should say one last thing. But what? Madly, I talked about the coat. Yes, it had belonged to Liliane, my guide, he said. 'I have aged with it. She wore it in her Manhattan life.' And he tapped my face and laughed. Peter Jack got a quick handshake and he was gone.

I sat drained, speechless and, as always, I wanted to run after him. *Stop in the name of love.* The film prospect did not look good.

Whatever I did, I must not remember how he was in the past or life could be dangerously incomprehensible.

Peter Jack, quite transformed, sat back excited. 'He is not what I expected.' I asked what he had expected.

'But he's a master. The most spiritually evolved man I have ever met.' So I hadn't got that over in the book. What else was left out?

'He is on a high spiritual level. A lot of work has gone into that,' Peter Jack said.

I didn't think I could bear to hear anymore about the person who had just left. And who could tell when he would appear again? There was so much left unsaid. I told Peter Jack we should plan a route back to the hotel and eat there. He pushed through to the door and said to give it a little longer. We agreed something so extreme could not last. We also agreed 3 Piece was a surprise. 'Didn't say one word. Didn't have to.'

Peter Jack was excited by him. 'He had real power and didn't need to do one thing. Just let his presence do it for him. I wouldn't like to get it wrong with him.'

'Dangerous?' I asked.

'He's the most effective guy I've met lately.'

Peter Jack was back to the reflective person I'd known in London. He was corporation and had to survive in that world but had other more subtle sides than his TV colleagues. Unlike them he didn't use the language of dissatisfaction, the reducing of everything to a common negative.

He asked if I placed the Dali card on the table for a purpose. 3 Piece had looked at it as though it was a sign. Peter Jack had seen his face, I only the profile. He didn't ask what José and I said about this meeting and for that I was relieved.

Before we left I asked the waitress what she would do with the photograph. I didn't think they put that sort of thing on the mirrored walls. 3 Piece must be a politician. Someone they needed to please.

'But he's not from here.' She was a little shaken. 'I only took the photographs because the man asked me to. I am sorry, I should have asked you. I thought you knew.' She did look sorry.

'So, he gave you the camera. Did he say why he wanted the photographs?' She shook her head. I didn't like this angle. 'Who is he?'

She didn't know.

'But you must know.'

'I have never seen him before. He is not from around here.'

He'd cut in on our meeting that we'd fixed up with our time and Peter Jack's money. It was not without difficulty getting hold of José and this man had imposed himself at the table and ignored us. Yes, we had been badly treated. That's probably what he did in his life. Silenced people. Gave orders.

The rain smacked us back into the doorway. 'At least there's no lightning.' For this I was grateful. We pushed out into the street. There was lightning.

4

When it did stop raining, I took Peter Jack to the French woman's garden with its two remaining walls on which the imprint where the tower had been was still visible, as was the outline of the staircase to the top floor of the house. A broken wall adjoining at right angles must have been part of the tower, we decided, and had a niche, perfect and untouched which would have held an artefact or lamp.

'So where was the door on street level?' Peter Jack liked to see sets that he was going to work with, as described. He had read both books thoroughly and had got the sense of the house. It just didn't fit what he now saw. 'And the room with the long table where Cocteau held the ritual?'

Yes, where was it? I had no explanation. I realized only that it felt more different than usual. It was all garden and no house. The city wall still in place which made up one side of the property pleased him. I got him on the wall for the views of Canigou and before he started asking where the royal palm tree had been, I said we would go to Ramon Masia's bookshop for original old photos of the actual tower.

'So where was the palm tree?' He had to ask. 'I don't see a place for it.' Nor did I. Before we left Girona , I went alone to the Arc bar, taken over by Luis, the eldest son of Luis, the Wolf, now deceased. I hadn't brought Peter Jack on this visit because I was not sure, any more, how those involved in the mystery of Girona would react.

What part did any of them play? Who were they? The archaic society was the core of the metaphysical activity, but when did its members show up in the light of day? Over the decades, the society had a more, and sometimes less, presence and my knowing any of it was due to my relationship to José. I knew his role of initiate and then custodian held him captive to the city. I had known a lawyer, Fernand Folch, who had been more open in the role and women with influence now in their 80s. In the 1970s, when José owned the Kabbalah Centre, Freemasons used to visit at night, and it was said by the waiters, they carried out ceremonies using the Sunstone. And the chronicler of the cathedral, the aged and much loved Doctor Marquez, had told me a little of the society and its influence in the 30s so confirming its somewhat ghostly existence.

It was about this time when I had met 3 Piece that I noticed I had changed, as though a virus of suspicion was waiting in this beloved city to claim me and make my spirit less. I should no longer trust. Be careful with new information, share less, ask more. It did not fit with my nature. As I walked up the Calle Forsa to the bar I had known since it opened in the 1950s, I wondered how Girona would react to the possibility of Peter Jack's film. After the meeting with José and 3 Piece, I'd have said not too well.

Luis Junior, the new owner was a surprise. For a start, he was so unexpected in a Spanish bar. Delicate, beautiful, he would be a perfect French movie actor belonging in superior places. He had a finely drawn face across which expressions appeared and faded, understated, always to the point. His origins remained undisclosed, his intelligence too high for the territory. About his emotional life who could guess? I asked him about 3 Piece, and what his role was exactly. My description meant nothing to him.

'Younger than José', I added.

He asked if the man spoke Catalan and I said I didn't hear him speak.

'For a writer you don't overdo description.'

An imperceptible shrug, a quick twitch of a smile, 'I do not know this man.' So I asked about the society.

'Be careful,' he said. 'My father would have been cautious around these people. He always looked after his friends. He would take care of you.' His eyes were dark and soulful as he remembered the past. 'If I find out anything about the man in the three-piece suit I will leave you a message.'

His eyes rested on mine with the full power of their sombre depths. How I wished I was a little younger, like 20 years.

His face was pale and wistful in the semi-darkness. 'We are both in something we don't understand. We always are.' His hand reached for mine and held it, the touch beautiful. 'Be careful.'

Yes, we were always on the outside.

Shortly after returning to London , Peter Jack said he was going back to Girona. He needed to get the feel of the place. I thought that was what he had been doing. He needed to go alone. Did I mind? He needed to experience it in his own way. I told him to have a good time. I told myself I did not mind.

He was back within a week and seemed to think he should account for himself. He had made a few small journeys and not seen José. A lot of time was accounted for in the French woman's garden and he knew now why there had been a recent problem in recalling how the layout had been in the 50s. The house now seemed so much smaller. Two floors? Not these days. The imprint of a sloping roof made the house as squat as a rabbit hutch. He had the explanation. 'They filled in the whole ground floor with earth or some filler so it starts now at the first floor. So the whole house and garden begin one storey higher. That is why it's confusing.'

It took a moment for that to reconcile with what I had recently seen.

He said that was why the street door led nowhere but to the garden steps. The root of the palm tree was not where you would expect. 'They filled it in. It's landscaped.'

'They?'

'The society.'

'Why?'

'To confuse.'

5

Early spring 2010, the publisher asked me to put together a tour of Girona for the Theosophical Society and associated groups. That increased to several groups as my research had opened up new territories in the esoteric world and general readers wanted to take the journey to the Portal site. Some would come anyway because they wanted to test the veracity of the material. I was to lead these ill-assorted groups and show the process as it had been given to me and also include a tourist visit to Girona's historical sites. I could think of nothing worse. Guiding tours was a new departure in my life but my agent said it would sell books. I was still doubtful so he said I only need do this till Peter Jack got the film underway and he had already front money in place. There was a definite shift to Catalonia. Troubador, Ani Williams and writers Kathleen McGowan and Filip Coppens suggested I be guest speaker on their summer tours which now included Girona. A popular interviewer on a US research channel suggested making a promo and Andrew Gough from the esoteric *Mindscap* magazine, filmed an interview in Girona with me and some of the protagonists from the story.

José was not available. In fact he was less visible than at any time in all the years I'd known him. Either the society or his wife had suggested he keep out of what could become a dreaded deluge of curiosity.

In the last few years I had seen José mostly at the time of the flower show and we would meet at exactly the same place at a precise archway in the old German garden and always by chance. It could be any day. Nothing was pre-arranged, not in an earthly sense. And after a while I noticed it was before the bells rang for noon. I would sit resting on a bench and suddenly there would be a pause, no one around, no sign of activity, just the sound of the trees in the wind. Then I would hear footsteps, unique, unforgettable and he'd come through the arch to where I was sitting as he had the year before and the one before that. And he would shrug and laugh, his eyes bright and everything in place, all there as it should be. It was as though he had arrived through a Portal.

I privately hoped this first tour would coincide at least with the preparation for the flower show. It did not. The guests were allowed limited time and expenses and by agreement this first group was small. On the way to the French garden Andrew Gough unexpectedly appeared. He had been shooting some footage on the coast and was just passing through Girona to visit a church near the frontier. Did I know about a society 'La Sang'? I did not. He joined the group up towards the cathedral and discovered the fish symbol. It was engraved on steps and a fountain. Had I noticed it?

I had not. He knew what to look for.

'The fish is the first Christian symbol.' He confirmed the engravings were remarkably old and surprisingly little damaged by time. He located immediately the eight-petal flower also visible on walls and stairways and again the stones were considerably older than stated and yet had survived. With him on that short walk I started seeing afresh what had just been background.

Tall, well dressed and purposeful, seemingly always at his best he managed a radio programme with writer Filip Coppens and knew most of the esoteric community. Born in Chicago he lived in Richmond, London with his English wife who looked like a young Marilyn Monroe which drew a certain amount of attention and some envy. I understood he worked in communications for a US company. He had a good sense of humour and enjoyed life and was immediately popular with the group. I thought he'd be a much better tour leader than me. Engaging them effortlessly in conversation he continued walking with us and I suppose he was curious about what I was doing and where.

The arch of the French woman's garden had an inscription engraved into the stone, 'The House of the Canons'. He asked why Maria Tourdes, young and attractive, had come from France to live here if it was an ecclesiastical house for men. I explained the church had sold it off and the first secular owner built the tower in 1851. I added, the man probably needed to build a tower, and so bought the house. Was there a tower in Rennes-le-Château at the time?

According to material from Cassini, the map maker to the King of France in the seventeenth century, there were two towers – one in Rennes , and the other, Girona. There was further mention of their purpose in the eighteenth century. 'Why was the house and tower pulled down in the 1960s?' Andrew asked. 'What was supposed to come in its place?'

'Nothing.' I told him about El Americano and the search for documents in the stones.

'Somebody must have paid well for this to just happen and no explanation given. Yet it is still a garden in her memory.' He pointed to the plaque – 'The Garden of the French Woman' , 'Why would they remember her?'

I didn't know. 'I should sharpen up my questions.'

'You should.' He touched the stones of the arch. 'You just get told some of it. You're not in touch with the real power.'

I thought what he said was a warning and the truth.

He left to drive to the frontier and alone with the group I arrived at the Barraca, the hut on José's land behind the cathedral, point one of the Portal journey. We sat in meditation healing the past. I lay back on the grass and supposed I was facing the sun because I was aware of bright light. Then I saw a huge crane structure with metal slats along its arms and it took a moment to understand this must be in my mind as my eyes were closed. It stretched from within my consciousness far off towards the city and I was amazed how far it did reach and how vivid this image was. It was imprinted on my mind, not made up from the ever-restless, changing imagination. And then the structure slowly moved, so one end dropped and rested on the ground near me, providing a vast ladder reaching up skywards, the metal slats like rungs. I did not think to open my eyes. It was yellow and continued into a distance I could not fathom, and far off at the top were beings that moved in unison, quite peaceful, coming down the steps, and up. I looked at it all quite calmly as though it was the most natural thing that should happen, and I was drawn in my mind towards it and started, in my thoughts, to climb. I was definitely drawn out of myself and the Barraca was a mere box below. And then I realized I might not get back, that I did not belong with these calmly walking beings. Higher now, this part of myself, my consciousness climbing, the part that went through Portals, that attuned clairvoyantly, everything focussed on that, my body forgotten. Too far now, I cried out for help and sat up on the grass. Opening my eyes was not easy. First, there was no sun, second, there had been no sun. The others still sat in meditation seemingly untouched by my experience. In panic now I just left them without a word and I hurried to the woman who would assess the experience. Carmen Arago had helped me with the research into the secrets of the city. In her 80s, frail with young, vibrant eyes filled with expression and life, she took my hand and led me up the stone stairs of her exceptional house, rapid as a mountain goat. This was the palace of Nachmanides, the renowned scholar. The reception room at the top of the tower had views on all sides and a terrace shielded by a tiled roof on supports in the medieval style.

'Jacob's ladder,' she said immediately. 'That's what you witnessed. How wonderful! It is seen at this time of year around the Barraca.' She looked at me surprised. 'But it's something to celebrate, not to fear.'

When I got back to the garden the group still sat, though less meditatively. They looked at me curiously. At least I'd come back for them. It was the least I could say. It was one hell of a start as a tour guide.

6

Lewis Doyle, the high priest of metaphysical validity, wanted to be right on the spot when the next person went through a Portal. As he put it, he would bust the secret wide open. 'There are no secrets. Just ineffectual people who mind their own business and ruin their character.'

I told him not to come. I had seen him in action when my book, *City of Secrets*, came out in Girona.

'You need me. I am your guardian angel. Someone has to be. You've got to cover your back.'

'Who from?'

'Enemies. You've made some.'

Did he mean the society? He meant the characters in Rennes-le-Château, who were trying to kill off my work.

'You cannot imagine what they say about you on my programmes. I am the one, the only one who has stood up for you.'

So I asked what exactly was their gripe, and he said they believed José had put me up for it or I worked for Spanish tourism. Some people thought Lewis Doyle worked for the CIA and I let that rejoinder pass. I couldn't tell whose side, if any, he was on. Lewis, of Italian extraction, came from New Jersey and his past seemed to drop off on arrival in the UK, and life began for Lewis AD 2000, if that information was correct. I'd heard he was a CIA agent and frequented esoteric cliques to be ahead with the latest discoveries. He was more curious about scientific progress in that field and if he could get hold of a friendly scientist, he did not let go. I was great for him because my work took the priest's story into another place and he had the die-hards protesting in Rennes, intent on protecting their beliefs and income, and the hidden initiates in Girona keeping out of the way and seemingly impossible to track down. Tracking down was his thing. I was a novice on this scene and had no idea of the disparaging reactions a newcomer could receive. At the book's presentation night in Girona, in 2008, his crew had filmed every wink of an enemy's eye. Did the bookshop audience believe me? Did he believe me? Either way, he was happy. He had stirred up controversy in his media world, and was jubilant to film me fallen or triumphant. He had the story. He had made it clear to me he was the knight on the horse, and I set for slaughter.

On that visit in 2008, he turned Girona upside down. He'd got into the bowels of Masia's bookshop (forget the basement, he could always go lower), and he gathered all that was hidden of interest. He had taken over from me. Some Arc bar members were pleased to meet this charming, urbane American and they talked his ears off and he was loving it. His media outlet in the US overflowed with controversy. José avoided him.

Lewis Doyle worked in real estate. His passion, he said, was the metaphysical world and he knew the top people. He blew apart the rest. He owned two radio stations in the US, a web TV channel, all devoted to the esoteric. It was rumoured he lived with a guru who owned several ashrams in India.

Bright and courteous, he had an impeccable veneer that made some people distrust him instantly.

He was short and wore lifts. The luxuriant hair was possibly part toupee. He was well exercised with muscles, that made his body resemble that of a bulldog. In certain moods, he looked like Sinatra. Three times married, he was as he said, the wrong side of 50, and had a string of models as trophy companions. The rumour in New York was that he had set himself up as a sex specialist in LA and that line of work had got dodgy and put him on a fast train north. I noticed he avoided talking about the past and did not like direct questions. 'I'm on my way, babe. José can't save you.'

It was the thought of Lewis Doyle back in Girona, not the society members that made me reconsider my role as guide.

7

Cynthia had survived a comfortable, over satiated life in the Cotswolds and wanted adventure. In her well-disguised late 50s she decided on a new start. It may have been reading my books that persuaded her 'on the edge in Catalonia' was better than 'drowning in repetition in Moreton-in-Marsh'. At least, that's what she believed. She had been to the right schools, married solid men and in her youth had been a successful model, Cynthia le Kouche. Lately, she had run women's groups, was active in WI in Oxfordshire and was used to speaking in public. She had a sturdy English presence that was reassuring. However, she was unsure about her present identity and had decided she might become a journalist. She wanted excitement, danger and I looked as though I might provide it. For many reasons I was no longer sure about holding events alone in Girona and she was a good companion and our interests did not clash. Of a certain age, that she held back with admirable effort, and might have succeeded if it wasn't for a liking of lemon sorbet, she had lost none of the visibility and verve of her youth. These days she liked drama but the everyday unscripted variety, preferably other people's, but in her own home if necessary.

On this spring morning, before my second tour, we agreed the heat was too much and we would shelter in the shade.

I did not expect to see José. It was not yet the flower show and the lovely moment by the arch in the German garden. But he was there, unmistakable, at the side of the track and seemed to be alone. It took a moment just to adapt to the fact that life or destiny had once again seen fit to put us together in defiance of what had been personally decided. His welcome was soft-voiced and it seemed appropriate for one short embrace disguised as a polite greeting. We moved apart and forgot to let go our hands and then I remembered Cynthia. The cathedral bell chimed twelve sonorously. She said the right thing. This was the moment and the day when Buddha and Jesus descended into the etheric world, the nearest to earth they came. She had a strong, clear way with words.

He understood some of it. 'Then it is right we should meet,' he said and would not let go of my hand. He said a little of what he was doing and I replied in kind. We walked towards the nearest bar and then he remembered his wife. 'Let's just be here.' And I sat on the piece of wall, purportedly four thousand years old, its lovely innocence taking my part in affairs of the heart, on my side, offering its cool stones for those lovers wearied and heavy from years of compromise. Still holding his hand I pulled him towards me. 'I haven't long,' he said and the stones rattled a little in protest. And then he gave in and sat beside me, talked of other years and the wind sighed happily and the walls softened to our touch. How many lovers had shared their confidences here? How full the old stones were with secret trysts and how discrete they would always be.

Then he remembered Cynthia. No, she did not understand Spanish or Catalan. I was surprised when she said she didn't know French. She insisted not and it went on surprising me. 'So, say whatever,' she said to me. 'I won't know a thing.' Like hell she wouldn't.

'No French at school?' She would have gone to the right school.

'All forgotten.'

I wondered if I'd told her José and I mostly kept our exchanges in French. The feel of the wall still cool in the sun made me carefree and I told him we should go away together and live in a house of stone and celebrate each joyful hour as it passed.

'We've tried that.' And as an offering to the moment he said this wall, sitting in the shade, was as good as it got.

'Things have changed, José. You were always the first to appreciate a novel idea especially when it was unlikely to happen.'

'But you need old stone. You won't leave Girona.'

I said stones meant nothing particular to me.

'El Pessebre — you cannot have forgotten that?' He looked at me and saw for now I had. 'The Cradle. You liked the feel of that stone.'

I asked if he was saying a cradle was made of stone. Had I misunderstood?

'The Stone Cradle?' He waited for me to acknowledge its existence.

Did he mean a black stone he had given me on a beach years ago? A cradle?

More a pebble. I was 16. Absent-minded I'd tossed it away and he'd picked it up quickly and pressed it into my hand. 'Don't throw your luck away.'

Much later, married with two children, I was coming back from a book publicity visit to Spain. I hadn't seen José for years. The same kind of stone had stuck in the wheel of the taxi taking me along the coast road to Barcelona airport. The driver had to stop in a deserted village and change the wheel. I crossed into the shade of a side street. Just one man leaning against a wall. Our eyes met. Marriage over. One black stone. No luck there. Did he ever think of that black day?

He was telling me now about a poem dedicated to the Cradle that he would present at a Cathar recital in the village of Sant Miquel de Fluvià. Neither Cynthia nor I had anything to add. I didn't remember any cradle.

'Perhaps mention of cradles stirs up too much in the past of what might have been.' Cynthia chose to speak in English into which a few French words had inadvertently slipped. Cynthia might have something there. In no language or three she was heading for drama.

His eyes did not leave mine. 'You used to lie in that Cradle and never wanted to leave.' I could see uncovering the past gave him more pleasure than anything in the present. Vaguely now I could recall a dark-blue smooth stone. Was it marble?

'One of the oldest in the planet,' he said.

'Monolithic,' said Cynthia knowingly.

'Palaeolithic. A meteorite,' he said.

She was going to ask where but he had changed the subject seemingly. 'You may have noticed that the valued secrets usually lie quite open and without disguise.'

'Why?'

'Because nobody had enough resonance to recognize anything. Hiding something draws attention and then they notice.'

Was he talking about the Cradle? Cynthia started to reply and remembered she didn't speak French.

Daily life was suddenly back. It shook through him, standing him up, all stones forgotten. His obligations had now been abandoned somewhere across the town. 'My God, I must hurry.' And our hands, leaving each other, took a little longer and I watched as they, with a will of their own, clung one last moment then slipped apart and the space that followed belonged in my grave.

Cynthia took the hand he had held and we walked back into the city. She was on my side.

When I next saw him some thought or impulse made me ask about 3 Piece. He took a moment and remembered the day of the deluge. He agreed he knew him. I said he seemed unfriendly. José frowned and decided on an answer.

'He has his preoccupations.'

I said preoccupied or not, he was hostile. I asked his name and what he did.

'Oh, he's not from around here.' As though that made it all right.

'Hostile.' I added, 'Intimidating.'

'Yes, he's not without a certain danger.'

That description of 3 Piece stayed. Even Cynthia had got the gist of that.

Ramon Masia had run the second-hand bookshop near the Arc bar since the mid-60s and I remembered he had been a performer at one time with a mass of hair, dyed red. He liked his hair coloured even now and the grey and white headstrong interlopers were instantly tinted scarlet. He was a cheerful man and his laugh covered many things. I was sure he went a lot deeper than a joke about the weather. He knew everyone in Girona and kept their secret belongings safely even after their death.

Over the years he had slipped me old letters and photographs helpful for research. He never talked of their origins or the people who frequented his store. A second-hand bookshop crowded with memorabilia was a good place for meetings of all kinds and in the darkened interior, dusty with deceptive light, men huddled in conversation and Ramon stayed at the front, keeping the tourists engaged with postcards and souvenirs.

He told me I probably did not need memorabilia anymore, now I finished the books. I agreed the subject was over. It was never over, but I didn't know it then. I asked about José. I always asked.

Ramon laughed. 'There is no one like him.'

Cynthia agreed warmly, her French not bad. 'He has a purity of spirit.'

In fact, her French was coming on in leaps and bounds. How modest she'd appeared with José. Surely she hadn't pretended not to understand the conversation so we would feel free to reveal all kinds of secrets?

'He should write his story,' she said.

'Oh, that will never happen.' Ramon sounded sure.

'If the price was right?'

'His story might be beyond price.'

And he lifted up a monstrously heavy tome from 1890 onto an impossibly full shelf and the dust puffed towards us. Coughing, she left. I stayed and asked about 3 Piece. Remembering Andy telling me to ask the right questions, I started on ones I might get answered. At the end I could only reply I was in a good place for secrets. I did ask who runs all this? The society? Of course, he didn't know. And the dust rose in defence of his argument.

I suggested to Cynthia she might be bilingual after all. Why hide it?

'If I am going ahead as a journalist, I had better be an active listener and not a second-class, showy linguist. I'll learn more.'

8

'Did you see 3 Piece?' Peter Jack always asked this when I came back from Girona. We were sitting in Lemonia having our usual enjoyable lunch and I realized we never talked about the script except to say he was getting on with it. He'd been doing that for some time and I'd never been shown a word. He'd not asked me any questions and that was rare too. In my experience most people in that business who'd optioned a book and were working on a script, usually asked too much. Peter Jack seemed to be writing in a vacuum with no outgoing lines to anyone. The one bit of news in the beginning had been the arrival on the project of a producer who had money and there was mention of a woman who might co-write. He'd paid the first option, we had taken our exploratory trip, he'd taken his solo trip and he was back in his study, presumably writing. Months had passed and I had left him alone. We respected each other's space. I trusted it and then I didn't.

I finished the halloumi and got ready to dive off a high board. The baklava arrived with the mint tea and I got ready for the high board again. Then I remembered José's words, 'This man will never tell my story. He will never make my film.' Had the script been cursed? Mouth too dry for words, I chose an easier way.

'Are you doing a lot of TV right now?'

'Bread-and-butter stuff.'

'Must take a lot of time, though.'

'Oh, it's predictable.'

'But it must take time away from writing the script. Our script.' No dive after all, just a splash in shallow water.

'No, I'm getting on with it.'

I'd heard that before. 'Can I look at a scene or two?'

He didn't expect this. Eyes a little sharp as he divided the baklava. 'I'd feel better to have it finished before showing any-thing.'

I understood that. 'But it's months.'

So he listed the work he'd had to do, the bread-and-butter kind and admitted it had taken longer than hoped. Was the producer still attached? Oh yes. No problem there.

'But you've got a first draft? All these weeks. Must have.'

'To be honest I've had a touch of writer's block.' Edgy, not enjoying the dessert.

'If there's anything I can do to help—etc.'

Yes, cursed. Both of us.

The bigger money was coming up soon, the continuation part of the option. Writer's block, bread-and-butter money, we'd see if he paid up then. He paid up. So everything was all right.

9

M iguel polished the thirteenth glass and placed it at the head of the table. Ani Williams, the well-known troubadour and harpist, had interviewed me about my work on *Reality Sandwich*, the US programme, and had brought a tour to Girona. She lived half the year in Sedona, US, and the rest near Rennes-le-Château and was considered the Grail-writer, Henry Lincoln's muse. Miguel, the young manager of the Blanc restaurant, adjoining our hotel, had made a success with a substantial three-course lunch for nine euros, and the place was always full.

'What do you do exactly?' Miguel asked. 'It's the Doorway isn't it? People die going through that.'

Was he talking about the Portal? He was.

'It's always called Daleth number four.'

I didn't expect this from the restaurant staff. I asked him if he was a Kabbalist, and he said he wasn't, but he'd got it from a man who studied Kabbalah. 'He mentioned you.'

So I asked who he was and he said someone vaguely familiar but he didn't know his name. 'I think you should consider why you are here.'

I watched him lay up the menus.

'The society may not like it. You draw attention to them.' I asked how he knew all this. 'Because I serve them a good lunch and after a few drinks they're all talking, and as I serve, I listen. They are not satisfied you are here or the manner of your being here.'

I wanted to know where the man who asked about me came from, and he said to look no further than the inner group of the society.

And all this coming from the boy who served my lunch. What else did he know? He laughed. What did I want? He said, 'You can be in Girona and know nothing about this. One, it's against the Catholic Church. Two, it doesn't fit in with the community view of the laws of this planet. To stand in one place where the surface of the planet is thin and goes through to another reality with extra dimensions – they don't like that.'

I stopped eating. 'Am I in danger?'

'Not from my food.'

'You know a lot about it.'

'Watch out for number 310. Or maybe 210. I will let you know.'

He didn't. The only 210 I got was the lunch bill for a group.

This conversation had never taken place.

I was aware of a cluster of men crossing the square, a sudden breeze rustling their crisp shirts. Ani had already jumped up and, shielding her eyes against the glare, pointed to the last man, now visible through the trees. He walked easily in this carefree hour, his elegant white hair lifting around his face, and as he moved, a light did seem to pass around him. Ani said, 'It is José.' And he came towards me bringing delight and radiance, all as it should be. He was brown, feet well on the earth, good in himself. 'He is better than anything I ever thought.' Ani was excited. 'He is made up of bits of light.'

Later, when we talked about the meeting, I was impressed she had spotted him so easily. 'Oh, he's not of this world. He is initiated on a high level. A poet. And that's just the hors d'oeuvre.'

When I introduced him to the group, they asked if they could take his photograph, and he allowed a pause and then agreed. He laughed with them. Why shouldn't he? He came from some magical place, touched by a life-joy we gravity-ridden ones could only acknowledge as it passed beyond us on its way. He liked Ani, and said he would come to her next recital. Age did not dim his charm.

Soham at her ashram in the Pyrenees had heard my Coast to Coast broadcast, and she wanted to know more about the Portal. Miguel, my new adviser on keeping alive, said it would be a good place to hide out, and I should accept the invitation.

From the US, Soham had gone to India 40 years ago and become the devotee of the Maharaji, and on his death would take over the lineage. She would be the wearer of the shoes. She still had enough beauty to make me imagine how her arrival all those years ago on the Ganges must have affected those gurus. However devout, they must have experienced a terrible rush of testosterone when they saw this perfect, voluptuous vision, with long golden hair rise out of the river. There would have been competition to claim her. Whatever actually happened, the Maharaji won, and she became his student and took his teaching around the world for many years. Today, the hair was still long and fair, the rest touched by God. Her French ashram served vegetarian food, good enough on its own as a reason to stay. Most of the time she was travelling across the world with her companion and driver, Holland , also from the States. The ashram was an undisturbed isolated land, the nearest hamlet 45 minutes distant. She was interested in the two towers, especially the one in Girona , and asked why it was pulled down. 'Because the perpetrators wanted the secret held by the society.' She asked what happened to the stones. I had never thought about that. No one had ever mentioned it. I understood the stones were hollowed and information had been hidden inside, and it was a skill learnt by the stone-builder guilds in the Middle Ages.

'They would have kept the stones,' said Holland . 'Taken them and rebuilt the tower.'

I had heard a lot of possibilities since publishing the books, some of them interesting, others were just 'others'. This sounded down to earth.

'How did they build the tower in the first place? And how would it be copied 200 km to the north-west?' His questions were friendly but snappy.

I understood they had used the golden section and Saunière had his architect copy the original Girona plans. Soham stopped me. 'No, Holland means the tower before? There would have been an older one.'

Liliane, my guide, said the early towers had been discovered by Cassini, the map maker, and he'd worked solidly through France until he got to the Perpignan area and had not been heard of for two years. Liliane said he had worked out the position of these towers using the stars.

'Who is El Americano?' Soham's voice only seemed soft. I had no idea. 'Hasn't it occurred to you who he might have been?'

It hadn't. Was she, like Andy, going to tell me I didn't ask the right questions? I began to see I was probably focussing on something obvious and missing the real point.

Was it just a Portal? I asked if she knew the identity. She said that a member of the Rockefeller family in New York on taking a liking to buildings in far places liked to have them dismantled, shipped to the States, and re-assembled. 'Remember knowledge is power,' she said.

Girona was crowded for siesta and I arrived at the bookshop, crushed and sweating, and asked Ramon for someone with information about El Americano. For once, he simply wrote a name on a bookmarker, 'The American Bar.'

'Anyone will tell you in the old bars,' and he pointed down towards the river. 'Anyone' would not tell me anything. This was Girona. The barmen were either too young, forgetful or too Catalan. The patron of the Peninsular Hotel remembered there had been a business of that name in the main square in 1933, when he first opened.

'It was a Spanish bar originally. I remember it suddenly changed its name because a stranger went in there and took a milkshake.'

Miguel was surprised to see me back, but I had at least one tour to prepare. He had never heard of El Americano.

Was El Americano the aviator NASA had asked me about? The man who replicated Portals after visiting the Pyrenees? I did not bother asking my agent, knowing his opinion of that call but went through Xochi, the PR at the American publisher, and she tried contacting NASA but I didn't even remember the man's name. I did a phone interview for a US talk show network and the host was married to a CIA agent, descended from the Hapsburgs.

'Aren't you afraid? You've opened all this up which has been covered up for years, and maybe the hidden society don't like it.'

No, I hadn't felt afraid. She said she would and had spoken to her husband who thought I had reason for fear and should re-consider my priorities. When we were off air, I asked if she had heard of El Americano, associated with Girona. She said she would find out, and I should stay close to my material, otherwise others would. She meant Lewis Doyle.

I walked into the bookshop and before I even asked my ques-tions, Masia handed me a magazine dated 1968. 'A man left you this.' Printed in Madrid, it featured Girona – 'the most beautiful and little-known city'. The photos were taken earlier than '68 because the French woman's property was still there. I could see the tower but not the house or palm tree. It seemed the property defied all photographs and it stayed swathed in secrets. There were photographs from the end of the nineteenth century show-ing the priest from Rennes-le-Château with guests in the garden, but these sepia snapshots did not find their way into out-of-date magazines. At the end of the ten pages, there was an article on Howard Hughes. What had he to do with Spain? I asked who had left it for me, and why.

'The magazine might tell you the answer. The man is from Ripoll. He used to be a priest.' Masia avoided looking at me as he sold postcards across the counter.

'Does he have a name?'

'Doctor Arnau.'

I asked if I should speak to him. Masia said why didn't I look at the magazine. Did he mean I had to read through all these pages in Castilian Spanish? He prodded at the cover and said there was an easier way. He even translated the Spanish so there were no mistakes.

'The city that no one knows' and further down, 'The man with everything seeks only one thing – a place where he is not known.'

So it was Girona. So Howard Hughes was El Americano. Maybe?

I asked to speak to Doctor Arnau and Masia dialled a number and gave me the phone.

The man had a measured voice, gentle and educated. He

remembered me from the early days of my Girona life. He was then an ecclesiastical scholar working at the cathedral, a close associate of Doctor Marquez. I did not remember him. He now lived in Ripoll. He said only a special being would appear as I had in the Calle Forsa in the mid-50s, dressed as a young waif. I had the gift of seeing, he said. I could have told him, not these days so much, as I hadn't seen the point of the magazine. He said we would speak again and was gone. I asked Masia if he was a retired priest.

'He is the most revered man, in a very high position.'

10

Lewis Doyle arrived in Girona, fresh from 'busting open' a counterfeit claim in Rennes-le-Château. Bones in a cave were said to be those of Mary Magdalene, and artefacts, produced only too recently, surrounded the skeleton to support the claim. Further evidence that a divine being had been taken to the area was deemed contrived by Lewis, who then extracted confessions from the would-be fame-seeking group. Consumed by a sense of justice, he turned his attention on Girona. 'I'm used to the wannabees, the hoaxers, the bullshit that Jesus married Magdalene, but I don't like these fly-by-night frauds, who raise hope and waste time. I deal with those.' He looked at me, and I was relieved that the Girona story had never included Mary Magdalene or Jesus.

'The lady with the cup — *la donna con la coppa*' had made appearances since medieval times. She had been variously painted and written about since the twelfth century. The initiates, having completed the journey to the Portal, could make space for her to pass through to our earth, always to heal. Her last sighting by some hundreds of inhabitants was in 1976.

I had the impression Lewis felt about this ethereal lady, much as a stalker did about a vulnerable woman out alone at night. He would smash this cloud of heavenly particles as he would a soap bubble blown by a child. I never knew if he listened to any of my assertions and always felt his interest was elsewhere. His enemies fought back on his social media, making slights about his appearance. He was an easy target. The latest, 'Don't listen to Lewis Doyle. He keeps his brain in his toupee.'

He called my room from the hotel foyer and made it clear he was still the knight on the horse, and I was set for slaughter. He said, 'Tell me what you want. I'm on your side.' I said I already had a producer, Peter Jack. Did I? He was the most silent film guy I'd met. I didn't try to avoid Lewis and felt his purpose was to finally meet José, but as people have said over the years, José could sense danger at 40 yards and quit the area in 4 seconds before it arrived. You can waste a lot of time trying to arrive in his vicinity. Where he was, he never is.

Lewis certainly had success with some women and was good looking in a B movie way. In the end, nobody trusted Lewis yet many fell in love with him.

He did a surprising favour and kept me from a head-on meeting with José's wife. Before I'd even seen her, he swept me into a doorway and made as if he was embracing me. 'You don't want to tangle with her,' he whispered. The wife did pause, not quite sure, then carried on up the street. 'She's worse than the Rennes lot.'

I asked how he knew her.

'I know a lot of things, babe. She would shove you ass-up down a Portal given the chance.'

It turned out he got his information from the Arc bar.

'I thought you didn't believe in Portals?'

'Oh, I certainly have no doubt about Portals. And the one on Canigou, where a being from another planet simply walked through to this one. Dali experienced this on Perpignan station and was never the same. But you haven't got it. The story goes much further on than a Portal. They've given you this to fob you off.'

So I asked about the 'they'. 'The society.' I asked why they fobbed me off. 'If they take me so seriously?'

'They want what you've got. They think you know more. So do I.'

He smiled with his dazzling teeth that were said to cost 150,000 bucks. 'Now let's go and have lunch with your Kabbalist friend, Katy. There is nothing to hide, sweetie. I'd like to get acquainted. I'll give you a tip. When you hear 5351, take it very seriously.'

He met the Hungarian Kabbalist by default. It was always his intention and I found out later how much he needed to satisfy an intention. I told her he was an unknown quantity and she asked for his date of birth. I don't know if that protected her. Everything was always numbers with Katy. 'Whatever you do, don't let him into your house.'

'I can look after myself,' she said.

She lived in a forest above the coast and had spent 30 years developing a spiritual life, studying Kabbalah, researching all aspects of the esoteric compass. She was thorough and totally reliable, and had many students. She was robust, healthy and looked younger than 78. She was sitting at a table outside the fish restaurant on the beach, wearing a blue gown and silver pendant and her fair hair was tied back. The two of us walked towards her but she saw only one. Her eyes as she looked at Lewis Doyle became bluer than any sea. They filled with light as half-murdered dreams struggled back to life. The eyes claimed the happiness fate had once promised. As she smiled at Lewis Doyle 50 years fell off her face and she became a girl in love and I watched this, which could only be described as a miracle, one I never forgot.

How he looked I couldn't see but he swung his body quickly into the most optimal seat and I was forgotten. It was a replay of the scene from the legendary film *Sunset Boulevard*, Gloria Swanson had not done it better. Don't let him into your house. Try stopping her. I was the one that didn't make it inside. They arranged he should fly back to her the following weekend and she would allow him access to her vast collection of esoterica. I told him practising secret rituals wouldn't be the full story. He'd have to do the more earthly kind. He laughed. 'I would swap sex for a Portal any day.'

She did teach him sacred symbols, allowed him to access etheric presences, and he had the fullest access to everything in that house. She did start his interest in transformation. I, with my little Portal work, was no longer in the picture. Lew, as she called him, was now on the map of her sacred alignments where the planets reinforced hers and his holy positions so they became the teacher and the beloved pupil, the Goddess and the lover-son. Reincarnation came into it. Jupiter and Ra and other ancient deities. How I laughed but I wasn't laughing inside. He'd taken her over and nothing was left for me. Did I learn from this? Did I heck.

One day he was gone. Katy died the following year, they said of a broken heart.

'I only leave good tracks,' he told me during our first quarrel after her death. He didn't leave any. That was the problem.

Luis had taken me out of the Arc bar, out of earshot, even from the waiters but kept his voice low. 'Earlier I was driving to the bar and just reached the Church of Saint Felix, and I couldn't believe what I saw. I nearly crashed the car. I thought, this is impossible. I must go to a psychiatrist. I decided the best plan was to get round here to the safety of the bar. I thought I had gone mad. I told my brother: go and look at the three windows by the church door.' He paused. 'Have you noticed them?'

I had not.

'My brother came back and confirmed what I have seen.'

Luis took my arm and walked downwards on steep, tricky cobbles under the arch to the huge Church of Saint Felix, which housed the sarcophagus of Saint Narcis, patron saint of Girona. We stopped in front of the main door and he gestured at three pointed arched windows. Each had a matching design, a floral centre outlined with black lines. Nothing to worry about here. He watched me while I looked at each window. There was some crisscrossing of the lines but the result was innocuous. 'You don't get it, do you?' I didn't get anything accept regret that I wasn't 35 years younger and somehow compatible for this charismatic bar star. So he told me to just let my mind take in the design. We were in crossword puzzle territory here, so I would never get it. So he helped a little and said, stop thinking flower and petal and look at the lines. Start lower down and take your gaze upwards. I got it. I was looking at the face of Satan, no argument. Three windows, three demonic faces of a beast, long and undeniable. I started to laugh. And from that moment the windows were only satanic and I never saw the floral interpretation again.

'Same for me,' he said. 'I expected flowers until the moment I didn't. What a place this is that has three satanic windows in a Christian church.'

It was such a simple design, the lines and curving petals made the most powerful demon I had seen—part creature, part beast, with a long central aspect on its face, which seemed to dominate and was utterly without mercy. It just existed for its own purpose and not one for our benefit. It seemed everything led from that long central face and it had no eyes or was blind. There had to be some explanation or solution. 'They had a good one,' Luis said. 'They'd simply boarded up those windows for 200 years. They recently uncovered them but don't know what they have. So that's the City of Secrets for you.'

11

There was something unnerving in the room yet the furniture was as before, the objects untouched. It was as though something else existed in this space, a presence I could not recognize. I did not have the everyday perception of time and it was held up, its tension increasing, becoming almost unbearable. The nearest I could liken it to was the period just before starting giving birth. I phoned Doctor Arnau in Ripoll and why I could not tell. I said the hotel room had an unusual feel.

'If you are a medium, as I'm told you are, then you must be used to picking up atmosphere at the very least.'

Had an occupant from this room passed into spirit and returned? I mentally covered my body from the top of my head to the soles of my feet with gold light to shield myself.

José Tarres used to say, 'You were born with the gift of seeing and were given the amulet of protection.' Doctor Arnau waited for me to reply.

'Hope so.' Mouth dry.

'What are you doing in Girona when you have your children to look after?' Jumpily I explained they were grandchildren, although come to think of it, I looked after all of them. I drank water from the bottle.

'Exactly,' he said. 'Your granddaughter.'

This was the last thing I recall him saying. Had I told him about my granddaughter? There was, beyond doubt, something wrong with room 206. It was as though an electric device was left on, a charger, a machine sending vibrations, disturbing energies into this small ordinary space. I checked the clock. It was still innocently ticking. Why did I think the hands were going backwards? I dropped the clock and pulled out all plugs from the sockets.

Had some person come into my room and gone, just as I was about to arrive? Had they left an atmosphere? A faint perfume? A desultory intention? This interloper had searched my belongings? I checked my passport and credit cards.

I rang José. 'I have not got the real story, have I?' I was reminded of Lewis Doyle's cautionary words, 'What you gave me was not enough. Who is Doctor Arnau exactly?'

He still didn't answer. Then his voice, unlike any other, saved me. 'Just breathe deeply and slowly.' He was onto it. He sensed the wrongness in the room.

'Think of the clear crystal light on that day we went north to the frontier and there was a hamlet on a hill with views on all sides.'

'But that was years ago.'

'And we will never forget that light. Unearthly. And I gave you the key. I said "This is yours."'

I did not remember.

'I told you to keep it for yourself. Never tell of that place.'

'Was it valuable?'

'I wouldn't have given it to you otherwise.'

A key? Did I still have it?

'Not a key in the usual sense. This opens a different kind of lock. The light pale-blue crystalline. Never forget.'

'Some say Doctor Arnau is the custodian of the society, the one you looked after years ago. I should ask him why he gave me the magazine.'

'He is impossible to reach and would not be bothered with this. He's away in Paris.'

'He sounded bothered, even in Ripoll. I just spoke to him.'

'Maybe you should go home.'

'Home? No, José, you gave me the material and said write it, because you thought you were dying and you presumably trusted me and then you backed off leaving me with the stories half told. That is dangerous. Take a side.'

'I want a peaceful life.'

'I need to know the real story.' A longer pause, then I asked if this was dangerous.

'You have finished with it now. You've written the books.'

I asked him how you knew if someone was an initiate. He said he was sure that Liliane had explained that. 'You wouldn't go around saying "I am an initiate". What you had passed through would speak for itself.'

'So you don't declare you are an initiate?'

'Only if you're an idiot and therefore not one.'

So I told him the number Lewis Doyle had given me, 5351. 'Is it a date? A code? A Vatican bank code?'

Again, he cleared his throat. 'I do know we come from a place of love and it just gets compromised. Remember that.'

12

The next day José was raking earth in the French garden. He still took the responsibility of looking after the property that was open to everybody, its purpose known to few. Anna, my Norwegian friend who had done much of the research, came with me. A psychotherapist she spoke excellent French and saw him from a different angle. I wanted her to translate his answers. I wanted no mistakes.

'The tower was pulled down by who?'

He went on with the raking and didn't want to answer. I gave him a few possibilities and he didn't accept these. 'Was it El Americano?'

'Of course.'

'Who was he?' I was giving him a chance to tell me. More shrugs.

'You never mentioned Howard Hughes.' I asked why he had come here.

'He'd already been here.'

This was a surprise. 'Here? What did they say here?'

'What should they say? They didn't know him and he didn't just come and say "I'm Howard Hughes". Would they know anyway?'

'When was it?'

'1933. You should have asked Doctor Marquez. He met him.' He stopped the raking. 'You should ask Narcis at the cathedral. His family looked after him.'

'Did he come alone? Why? What for?'

'He came for the same reason as Hitler and other Nazis and the Hapsburgs and the Arabs, Saunière, Wagner. He was with Otto Rahn, the German writer seeking the Grail.'

'So what did Hughes do here?' Anna asked

'It's said he came to the Barraca to see the first site of the journey and then onto the mountain.'

'To the Portal?'

For José that was obvious.

'Did he do the journey?'

'I don't think so. He went to Scotland and bought a boat and renamed it the *Southern Cross*, which is the name of the constellation, south of the equator. And he sailed there and did the initiation in his boat under the constellation and then he went back to America and after the Second World War employed German scientists to research the Portal on Canigou and replicate it in the States. Hughes made one mistake — strange after his childhood of illness. He didn't include a quarantine in his artificial Portals and it went wrong. There was a disaster with a ship. It was made into a film.'

Of course, the aviator NASA had asked me about. 'Did you meet him?' I asked.

'How old do you think I am?'

José knew a great deal about it. I had known nothing. I asked why Hughes pulled down the house.

'Not him personally. He sent men to get the material belonging to the society.'

'But he didn't get it.'

'Not a chance. It was rumoured he came here in the early 50s when Ava Gardner was making *Pandoro and the Flying Dutchman* with James Mason on the coast. Hughes was always after her.'

He introduced me to Narcis who worked in the records at the cathedral. He was a man happy to talk about his past. 'I didn't meet him. My great-grandfather, a priest, friendly with José's family took him to the Barraca. He was with the German medieval writer Otto Rahn. They went to a bar. Hughes only drank flavoured milk. After his visit the owners named it the American Bar. They also went to the Peninsular Hotel, which had just opened. But they spent a night in my family home. My great-uncle knew him quite well, so maybe he stayed more days. He said El Americano wants to go further and faster than is possible into the sun and has no fear. Yet he sits in a room alone and trembles because he sees a cockroach.'

63

'Maybe they went to the Portal together,' José suggested.

Narcis said it was possible. 'Things happen in Girona and they are exciting and should be remembered but then they are covered over as though they never happened.'

I showed Narcis the cover of the magazine. '"The man with everything." Is it deliberate? A code?'

'Just chance,' said José. 'Or someone up there.' He pointed up.

'What did Hughes do with the stones from the house and tower?' I asked.

'Became disappointed,' said José laughing. 'They were empty.'

I asked if the priest in Ripoll would know more. There was an unusual silence. José without an answer? Hadn't seen that often. The two men didn't look at each other but they were in total agreement. Narcis got up and hugged me. 'I'd leave all this alone. I wouldn't bother going there.'

'He gave me the magazine,' I said. 'So he will talk to me.'

José clapped a hand to his head. 'How much worse does this have to get?'

Suddenly there was no priest in Ripoll, or Howard Hughes. Ramon Masia only vaguely remembered something but was too busy to talk. 'But the magazine — ?'

'Just a game. Like a treasure hunt,' he decided and said no more. The one thing about Girona, they sure could keep a secret.

The key to Howard Hughes wasn't in a magazine but right in my hand. Arve H, the Norwegian pilot, had known the aviator in the States and Arve was a friend of Anna and would know if anyone did, if Hughes had connections with Girona. Arve had a bold, generous life-filled drunken laugh when he was sober. Other times? Another story.

Girona? Only the film actress he was after. 'Ava Gardner. She was there. She said she never did anything with Howard.' More laughter. The laugh had lasted him over 70 years. 'Everyone does something with Howard even if it's to mix a milkshake.'

Anna warned me Arve could only be contacted before noon; after that, some drinking got in the way of facts. It was a little after the Cinderella hour. I had spent summers with Arve and friends at Anna's summer house on the Oslo fjord. He was big, tireless, got things right, and, however drunk, he couldn't get rid of his intelligence. He was an inventor, an adventurer, he did not know fear. Arve would take my hand to lead me down steep slithering rocks to the small unsteady boat and his grip was all enclosing, soft like blubber, huge and I couldn't release my hand. It felt as if it was held in the stomach of a whale. 'Hold on,' he'd say. 'Don't get ideas.'

'The water is not deep, Arve.'

'You can drown in shallow mud.'

Born in Tromsø in the north of Norway, Arve had been chosen at 17 to test US heavy jets. He was a phenomenal pilot and got the attention of Hughes who wanted Arve to work for him.

'It was in the late 50s and early 60s, but I continued with the air force. They were all linked together anyway. I used to go out with Hughes, but not for chicks. We spent all night talking about planes, and sometimes flying them. He was good. He wanted to fly faster, higher, further and go. I used to think: go where? The very edge.'

What he said echoed what Dr Marquez's relative had told me in Girona.

Arve went back to Norway in the early 60s and introduced the pizza. He opened pizzerias with nightclubs underneath. He made a fortune. He bought a magnificent car, drove to St Tropez and with Bardot, he turned Le Club 55 into an international hotspot filled with the rich and famous. Arve lived high and fast and never knew a quiet moment. Driving back to Norway he regaled the Oslo society with his conquests and wealth. He was never afraid to hide success and made enemies.

Jealous competitors looked him over for just one flaw. It did not take long. Arve never bothered to pay tax. 'I was banged up inside and Howard got to hear about it and offered me a job. I went back to the States working with the air force. I saw Howard from time to time and preferred to be a buddy, not an employee.'

He described visiting Hughes was not of this world. 'I walked into this bunker the size of lower Manhattan and it was filled with scientists, a German inventor, fortune tellers, soothsayers, hypnotists, the CIA, the Space Program, more inventors, construction workers, Jack Parsons and Howard would come down in his pyjama bottoms or top with the hair and the nails and create this – vacuum.' I asked what it was. 'Howard was holding back time. Through this aperture you could go out and come back the same age as when you left.'

'Was it a Portal?'

'He didn't call it that. He said "gateway".'

'Was he frightened the government would find out?'

'He was working with the government. They were funding him. One time he had to go and account to them for where the money was going. And the business of the ship – that was another problem. It disappeared for 40 years. He made a ship vanish for 40 years.' A good loud laugh on that one.

'Was that the Philadelphia Experiment?'

'You couldn't put it like that in those days. I said, "Howard, you can't go along to that hearing in those goddamn pyjamas" and I got him buttoned up into a suit and someone cut his hair and he looked sort of normal. He was never crazy. That's all wrong. He was bright to the end but nerve shattered and going at a too high frequency because of all his slipping through the aperture to those other realities.' He suddenly stopped and that was it.

I asked about Girona, Otto Rahn, Portals, his boat the *Southern Cross* and got nothing. Then he remembered the mountain. 'After the Second World War he sent the scientists who had worked for the Nazis to the French border with Spain. He wanted to measure the energy and copy the structure of the aperture.'

'Did he?'

'Well, he used something for all those goddamn invisible doors that made everything in you speed up till a cockroach looked like a dinosaur.'

Arve wasn't interested in apertures only planes.

A house and tower pulled down in Girona? A palm tree uprooted meant nothing to him. Stones with hidden cavities?

Had he seen them? I asked if Hughes ever just went off on his own?

'He did do that. He'd disappear for days. Sometimes by plane but he did like to walk and keep walking and no one knew where he was. He was a solitary man. Yes, he had this other side but I didn't see it.' The story for Arve ended with the mountain.

I was doing tours and not writing books. I was not doing what I wanted but the agent said the film would rescue the situation and I believed him because that had happened in the past. He was sure once the script was finalized the project would move fast. There came a moment when I finally put words to a disquieting uncertainty that had come and gone lately.

'The film would not happen.' Where were the usual signs of a venture on the move? The actress? Peter Jack never mentioned one. What about some healthy bad news?

Budget too high? Too low? Nothing.

Two women sat on the wall by the elaborate shrine to the Lady with the Cup but it had been switched to Jesus. The Saviour not the Lady had, according to the society, appeared in 1976. The recipients had got it wrong. Maybe these two women were devotees of the Lady with the Cup and her healing. One hundred met each month still firm in their belief. I asked the women if they were sitting in reverence?

'Sitting in the shade.' The one who spoke was handsome with a strong, beautiful face that would not age. The other fairer and more tender-featured had no such defence and her eyes were puffy. They were high-class and pleasant as far as I could tell. I asked them to move up because the heat was killing me.

They were sisters living in Girona and had known me for years. Had to get a senior moment check-up here. I did not know them.

'Our father was the custodian in late 50s. He was the lawyer, Fernand Folch. He liked you. You were such an elegant sprite.'

I hoped that's what she said.

'Fernand Folch—José was his assistant and did all the work. Then José took over later.'

'So you think there is a mystery in this city?' I said.

'But, of course,' they said together.

'So who has it?'

More laughter. 'You!'

It was enough to make me laugh. I wanted to know the present custodian.

'Doctor Arnau, in Ripoll.'

'Who is he?'

They had a little Catalan discussion. 'A theologian. A mystic. Like Jacint Verdaguer, he holds the way.'

'How do I get to him?'

'You don't. He comes to you.'

'Can you arrange it?' I was so hot, sweat dropped onto my knees. They weren't sure about that and the ageing one prodded the ageless one and they were going to turn Catalan and so, reserved on the subject.

They said Dr Arnau was a friend of José and was in his late 60s. His students adored him. He was sensitive, well-educated, an evolved being.

I turned to the subject of 3 Piece. However I described him made it worse. They had never seen this man.

'Yet another mystery.' They laughed.

13

My agent had become a dormouse and not much stirred him. I asked several times for news of Peter Jack, if the film was progressing. Finally, he picked up a phone and said it was still at script stage. Forget progress. The books had probably sold their quota. The mystery had subsided.

And then I crossed the path of the one who did know everything and we sat together in a private patio, in which everything was painted blue. I told José the story had just ceased. It seemed there was nothing else to find.

He opened his arms in defeat. 'The Portal. What else can there be?'

I said it seemed there was more. And then I remembered the key. Did I take it back to London all those years ago? How large was it? I asked again when he had given it to me.

He frowned, 'Things come and go with you.'

'I'll tell you one thing, José, I would never have given up something you gave me. What was it like? Is it a question of its price?'

'It is beyond price.' He was ready to go. 'It was yours for a while.'

'Why are you in this, José?'

'I was born in this.' He left through the shadowed doorway.

I sat down on a blue chair and facing me on a stone wall was a gilt plaque in Catalan honouring José Tarres for his restoring Girona and uncovering the golden era of Catalonia. He was a true initiate. It was signed by Doctor Mascaro who had died in 2007 and left this patio in José's honour. I remembered too much. I sat and would have cried for what had been and what could never be.

Suddenly there was nothing else. Maybe there was nothing. It had all been Chinese whispers. I sat in the Arc bar waiting for Kathleen McGowan and Filip. I could only hide the sadness and repeat the journeys to the Portal sites, much as Liliane had done with me.

Ramon Masia came in from the bookshop and took a coffee, picked up a newspaper and then saw me. 'How are you?'

'Absolutely fine.' I hate this fucking town. I haven't even had the rebirth. You listening, Liliane? If you are out of your grave and the wind is blowing fierce, whipping your white garments of death, then, listen up. You promised me rebirth.

Ramon Masia was looking kindly into my face. 'Have you been crying, dear Patrice?'

Cry? 'No. Allergy.' That relieved him enough to sit at my table.

For once I had nothing to ask him, no questions, no interest. I thought I should leave earlier but I liked Filip and Kathleen and would not let them down.

'How long are you staying this time?' He was being polite.

'Minimum.'

The silence was killing him. He would have to ask questions next.

'I saw you walking up the road with a large group. The woman with red hair.'

'She's a famous writer in the States. Famous everywhere. Only Dan Brown sells more.' Eat your heart out Ramon. You won't meet her.

'Girona's lively,' he said, desperate for conversation. 'Big argument during the flower show.' He waited for me to be interested. Too late. 'Someone wanted to rebuild the tower in the French woman's garden. José refused. José said: where was the money for the stones? So the man said he would build it in rubber'. He waited for me to laugh. 'For the flower show. And afterwards recreate it in stone. There was a design. José said it looked like Disneyland.'

'Who is he?' For something to say.

'A private man in this city.'

Aren't they always?

'So, why doesn't he just go ahead and build the' – leave out *fucking* – 'Tower?'

70

'I think it's a question of who has the power.'

'So José stopped it?'

'Seems so.' He nodded. 'And the other one doesn't like it. But how crazy can anyone be to build a tower in that garden?'

'Someone who tried to publish a book and make a film.'

Not understanding he blamed himself for his language limitation.

'Ramon, we are speaking in fucking Catalan.'

'José is someone of influence,' he said, proud to know him.

That could change. 'Please don't mention that person's name to me, ever.'

'You mean the one with the rubber tower?'

'He's the private one I don't know, remember?' I closed my eyes. Catalans were also foolish.

'Your allergy is worse. Your eyes. Shall I get something from the pharmacy?'

'Yeah, a new heart.'

He stirred his coffee, which was now undrinkable. He looked at me wondering if I had a real problem. Heart? I could see he wanted to help. He decided to cheer me up. 'It's funny how many Americans get into this story.' He thought he was changing the subject. 'Howard Hughes.' They always made it sound like 'huge'.

'And Doy.'

Didn't know him.

'The small American with the smile.'

'You're talking about 50 million of them, Ramon.'

'Doy. Loo.'

'Lew Doyle you mean?' A little interest there. Allergy may be drying up. 'Where did Lew Doyle come into this?'

'He was here.'

'Weeks ago. Last time seeing Katy.'

'Last week he came to the bookstore and went through everything. He said José was more important than anyone realized. He was Saunière's grandson. And the French woman his grandmother.'

I'd heard a lot in my life. This would have me laughing next. 'So what's important about that?' Pause. 'Was it possible?'

'Luis always said it was so,' he said.

'No one told me.'

'He has all the rights of the society. He says yes, no. No, to the tower.'

'He's always been closed, Ramon.'

'He has to be. It's the custodial role. He didn't even tell his wife. I don't think his son has anything to do with it. It's not just about physical things.' He started speaking again, unusually for him, 'It's above the physical things of the earth. Beyond human activity. He's had a responsibility — your —'

Was he going to say lover?

'Companion.' Frightened he'd said too much, he decided to leave. I'd never heard him say so much in all the years I'd known him. Amongst the words little sparks of fire that could have taken hold, become a flame but my unseen tears snuffed everything out.

14

Kathleen McGowan had written best-selling books, including *The Unexpected One*, that had given her a substantial following especially in the States. Sought after, she had easily assembled groups to see the source material of her books. She was Celtic to the bone, and seemed to have a natural strength that restored itself. On esoteric matters, she was pinpoint sharp and knew her stuff. Everything was researched, her core theme the Magdalene, who seemed to rise out of her books a little more defined than before. Her face, strong and sensual, varied with mood and chemistry, showed she had lived, challenged and survived. Her red, long hair was immediately noticeable.

I had known the esoteric writer, Filip Coppens, since 2007, and he believed I had got the link between Girona and Canigou right, but that the end place was Perillos, not Rennes-le-Château. He made several illustrations on his Perillos website why this is so. He also mentioned how Saunière surrounded himself with mirrors, and reflections had a certain significance in the mystery. If only I had taken note of that.

It was a large tour group and Kathleen didn't waste time. Two days in Girona to cover the territory and in a thick twisting line, coiling around the old streets, moving swiftly in the heat, we did not go unnoticed. At the Arc bar, we were introduced to the satanic windows. Kathleen couldn't get it at first and then she couldn't not get it. She discovered, as Andrew Gough had, many stones engraved with the eight-petalled sign and they pleased her. She said it meant harmony and perfection and eight was beautiful.

We realized we were eight going for meditation to the Barraca site, one of the journey, 'the hidden'. I called out to the guardian but the broom against the padlocked blue door signalled he was not there. We stood in a circle and at some points in the meditation, we became aware that the old ground of the Barraca yard was made up of circles of stones, and they gave an impression of turning and spinning, taking us with them, spiralling up off the ground for a few long seconds, defying gravity. The group assessed with ease the spirit of this hidden yard, became part of its retreat from everyday life, sensed its past. I suggested for the next meditation we form a figure of eight, and then two circles overlapping, making a *vesica piscis*, practices I had had to understand on the Portal journey.

'Eight again. It's perfect,' Kathleen said.

And then the Barraca door opened and the guardian in his ragged workman clothes made us nine. The usual sign of his absence was still in place, the broom against the lock. I made some greeting to him and told the group to keep going. And he just sat on the step as the bells chimed the half-hour, lit a cigarette and watched us. Eight and nine were definitely different numbers, I could vouch for that. I did wonder why he hadn't answered and, if he had been absent, how did he get back in as there was no other way except through the blue door? Nine was not eight and meditation was over. I told the group about the Lady with the Cup vision and on the insistence of the authorities it had been Jesus that had appeared. They would have written it off altogether but the Lady always left a mark like a lightning strike, a burned sign, apparently Daleth 4 Door, and they couldn't get out of that. Too many people had seen it.

'Who is he?' Kathleen wanted to know. I said the guardian. She said 'More than that?'

'Works for the society, possibly.' A dog howled and it made her alert.

'I just feel I'm watched here in Girona,' she said.

'So do I,' said Filip. 'It started around midday.'

'I don't think the title of your book *City of Secrets* even starts to do it justice. This is one secret—the whole thing—the landscape—the lot,' Filip said. 'And they know we're here and somehow where we're going next before we know ourselves.'

And I started to think a little more like Filip. I noticed the guardian, how he came in and out of that Barraca without allowing even a glimpse of that interior I knew so well. It was a very practiced move. I thanked him as we were leaving and as I climbed the steps he asked how old I was. 'You must be older than me,' he said. I would thank him a little less next time.

It was a full group the next morning which wound to a stop by the Arc bar hoping for refreshments. Kathleen wanted to keep moving and then I heard a man say my name. Looking around I didn't see anyone I knew. And then I saw him, a substantial man in a jacket standing outside the bar at the far corner by the furthest table. He wasn't exactly hidden. He wasn't a journalist, by now I knew most of them. He was carrying a briefcase. He beckoned to me and waited, expecting me to go to him. The whole group was silent, watching, hoping perhaps it was José. I stood my ground staring at him and he decided the only solution was to come to me and he stopped just before the table nearest to the group. He felt into the briefcase and produced a large envelope and again asked me to go to him. He extended his hand and I still did not move. He put the briefcase on the empty table and slipped out the contents of the envelope. He was nearer to me now and I recognized the power. The hair was different. He did not wear a three-piece suit. He gave me three photos, one by one and the last showed the scene in the Antigua bar. It wasn't about my receiving them but what he wanted. I nodded goodbye and started walking, the group behind me. I must have been shaken up because I took the cathedral steps, instead of curving around the side streets in the shade.

'It's 3 Piece,' I said.

Kathleen was beside me. 'Whatever you do, don't under-estimate that man.' She turned around to look at the Arc bar but he was no longer there. Filip asked if the man had left and turned and stared back down 40 or 50 crowded steps. We still had many more to climb.

'They're watching us,' said Filip. Kathleen, definitely uneasy, took the photos from me and showed them to Filip. 'It's a message,' he said.

I agreed. The first, young, at the top of my game, with Dali. The second, a little older and entangled with José again. (Should know better.) Third, much older and as a result of all the wrong moves, sitting in the Antigua bar with unknown company. This was not Hollywood.

Kathleen changed the schedule and gave the group two hours free time before visiting the cathedral. Apart from its highlights, including Charlemagne's Chair, the tapestry of the Creation, the Beatus Book of Creation, she would show them the paintings of the Magdalene arriving by boat at a nearby shore. Now she was interested, as I was, to track down 3 Piece.

Filip asked if I knew him and I described the wet afternoon at Café Antigua with Peter Jack.

'This morning he was waiting for you outside the Arc,' said Kathleen. 'With these photographs. Maybe he just happened to be there, but why not sitting down? And with a bunch of photographs of you? I doubt it.'

'He was standing, yet there were empty tables,' Filip realized. 'And he stood way off in the shadows. He knew you'd be there at that time. 10.15.'

'So, who knew you would be there?' said Kathleen.

'Only Luis. But I didn't tell him.'

'I bet on the bar owner, Luis,' said Filip. 'He's the "double". He fits the description. Hears. Sees. Knows. And he's got that careful manner. Doesn't give a thing away.'

'If he told 3 Piece you'd be there, be careful what you say to him. He could work for the society,' Kathleen spoke decisively. She could feel danger I couldn't even imagine.

Filip came with me to the Café Antigua. We showed the photograph of four at the table and the waitress didn't remember anything. She had not seen this man and did not know of him. Luis at the Arc looked carefully at the photograph as Filip looked at him. Delicately he pushed the picture away. 'I do not know him. He does not come here.'

'He did this morning,' said Filip.

'I had never seen him,' Luis dropped the smile.

'He was standing outside by the tables.' Filip was almost off-hand.

76

'That's what I'm telling you,' Luis was becoming impatient. 'This person does not come here.' He was now speaking to me. 'Who knows who is outside. Inside is enough.' He went away saying he was busy although the bar was quiet.

Ramon Masia had just opened his bookshop early and carrying sheets of printed paper rushed us outside. I had never seen him so excited. Pointing in the direction of the French woman's house he waved his papers. 'This has just become available, this minute.'

They were photocopies of a picture of the Magdalene in reverie by a tomb. 'It's the altarpiece at Rennes-le-Château,' Kathleen said.

'Yes,' said Ramon. 'I want to show you something incredible.'

He started walking fast up to the back of the cathedral and around towards the French garden. I wanted him to look at the photograph of 3 Piece but he was more interested in his discovery. 'It is incredible but I have known it all my life. You are the first to see it.' Locals followed carrying a ladder. Ramon went without pause to the still-standing corner where the tower had been, its imprint still visible and further along on the adjoining wall, a niche was clear as daylight. Ramon pointed. 'It was there.' He got up the ladder and placed the photocopy into the niche and it fitted. 'It is known as the altarpiece in Rennes-le-Château placed there by Saunière but no — it was here! This is where it belongs.'

I was truly impressed. 'When did it come here?'

'Either Saunière had it commissioned and painted here, or it was already here as a shrine in Maria's house. It is a bas-relief. People have remembered their parents seeing it.'

'Have you seen it?'

'I have seen it.'

'So, what's in Rennes?' I asked.

'A copy of what is here.'

'So there are two?' said Kathleen.

'A copy was made for Rennes-le-Château to be placed in the common-place all-in-one altar the priest had ordered in Carcassonne or Toulouse. The society did most of the churches,' said Ramon.

The famous altarpiece at Rennes-le-Château. Rennes and Girona are aligned with the dual towers, but also share an identical altarpiece

The group had gathered by the cathedral and the tour master would take them inside but on hearing of the discovery they came in little clusters to the garden and watched Ramon on the ladder. Then they did the only sensible thing. They took photographs.

'It does fit,' said Filip. 'And he knows about the altar.'

I held the ladder while Ramon got himself down. He was triumphant.

'So the French woman had the altarpiece that people thought originated in Rennes?' I said. 'What happened to it?'

'Before the house was pulled down someone came and took it for safekeeping.'

'It wasn't flat like a painting?' I wanted to be sure.

'It is as though sculpted. A bas-relief. And coloured.'

'So, it was in safekeeping when you saw it?' I said gently. 'Not in a chapel or—'

'In a private family estate.'

'So the Rennes one is a copy.' It couldn't be the original if that was in the French woman's property in this niche as late as 1964. 'Are you sure that people coming to the house saw it? Can I go and speak to their relatives?'

'Not possible. I am sorry.'

'Who is the family?' Kathleen asked Ramon.

'One of the oldest families in this province.'

'Can you say?' I asked. He could not.

Would the photocopy we all held tightly match the altarpiece in Rennes? In what way was it different? Kathleen had decided it was the same and when the tour was over she would go to Rennes to check it out.

Filip got up the ladder and fitted his copy into the niche. 'It changes the story of Rennes.'

Then I showed Ramon the photographs. He laughed at 3 Piece as though he was an old friend.

'But it's Gyp.'

'But it's Gyp.' That made it all right. There was no time to ask questions. He was in a hurry and Kathleen was leaving for Montserrat.

After they'd left I was straight into the bookshop. Who was Gyp?

Even about this, Ramon could be vague. 'He is a Templar. From a very old family.' So I helped him with some questions but got nowhere. I wouldn't leave the bookshop and I could see he and his daughter were becoming perturbed. What were they going to do with their new altarpiece discovery? They didn't know yet. I asked for Gyp's full name and she immediately answered but in the thumping of books being moved I couldn't hear properly. I asked her to write it down. She said he was a private person and she would have to get permission. It was only correct.

'The Rennes-le-Château mystery is never solved,' he said to me and hoped I'd take heart and leave. He kept laying cards across the cluttered table all with the number five.

'What does that mean?'

'It's a pentagram,' his daughter said snappily.

'Wear that and you are invisible,' said Ramon.

'Is that true?'

'Magicians use it,' said the daughter and went to open the door to let me out. It was already open.

'Look at old books of magic,' said Ramon. 'You'll see what five is. A cloak of darkness. You are there. You cannot be seen or people just don't notice you.'

'Who are these for?' I pointed to the pile.

'Gyp.'

I phoned Cynthia and she agreed we should quickly focus a new September group on this sudden, startling mystery. How could it be identical in two places? And why? Who had painted it? We would make a comparison between the one in Rennes and the bas-relief in Girona.

Before leaving for London I sat with Anna in the Arc bar waiting for a meeting with José. Another deluge day and the bar was almost empty. Luis cleaned the counter scrupulously and suddenly his eyes met mine quite unexpected and I saw an expression I could not define. It made me think of Filip. Was he a "double"? José went first to Luis and gave him a message and then to our table and smiled sweetly. He had held up well in the rain but I could see this day was one belonging to an elderly man. I offered him a chair but he couldn't stay.

'So why did you come?' said Anna.

'I had to give a message to Luis for his mother.' It was said as smooth as cream.

A message for his mother? She was onto that. 'You walk all this way in the rain. What's wrong with the telephone, José?'

'It's delicate so I give it personally.' More smooth cream but he was aware of Luis wiping the bar, not looking at us, just listening. Something about Luis worried him, I could see that. He didn't want to talk in front of him so I took him off to a corner near where Gyp had waited. I showed him the photocopy of the altarpiece. He frowned then got out his glasses for a better look. Anna, beside me now and Luis, looking up, watched from the bar.

'It's here. This altarpiece,' I said. 'Who has it? The original is with an old family. Why didn't you tell me about this?'

He looked at me puzzled, then again at the copy. 'But this is Rennes-le-Château. No, Patrice.' He quickly handed it back to me. 'Not this. Keep away from this.' And in spite of the rain he was out of the door and gone.

15

Perhaps too hurriedly, Cynthia and I prepared the tour for September. The black-and-white photograph had waited on my laptop screen and I had been too busy to notice. As I came back into the room later that day, the image seemed to command attention. Close to, it was only a photograph of a woman's back and a bouquet of flowers on a table. It had only seemed powerful. There was no sender's name. It turned out to be a short clip of film emailed that morning and I opened the file and got a developing interior journey along a short passage leading to a partial view of a hotel room. A bouquet of mixed flowers on a glass table and the back view of a woman in a black cocktail dress and high-healed shoes was all there was before the clip ended. I did wonder what it had to do with me. There was something depressing about the room. Then it occurred to me it had been sent by mistake. I scrolled further down and saw a message, 'Look at this, well.'

From the woman's hairstyle, I thought it was taken in the 70s. What did it signify? It was a sign? A code? The photograph was too bland. I forwarded it to Lewis Doyle and he was back in minutes.

'Nothing here. Definitely no subtext. It's 50s decor, and the woman's clothes no later than the mid-70s. The room is old fashioned. I'd say East European. Nothing special. She wears a ring. I can just see that. And it's a reflection. It's been shot looking into a mirror. Don't think there's anything in it. Bye, sweetie.'

The 'nothing special' got my attention. The clip was absolutely uninteresting but that in itself became interesting. Was that the point? Had it lost something by being filmed in reflection? Whatever its point, it became disturbingly uncompromising. The photograph was an alarm. Later I did examine it again, looking for what made it special. A date? A label? A reflection? A half-concealed photograph? The clip stopped before we were really into the room, and was dominated by the vase of flowers.

Lew Doyle called and said as I was worried he had worked a little more on the photograph. 'It took time but I've got the sender's name of the forwarded message. She shows up wealthy, married a couple of times, once to a duke, the other a banker. She knew Otto von Hapsburg, who died recently. Oh, by the way, she's Hungarian. Don't think there's anything in it but check further if you want. Currently she's out of reach in New York. Oh yes, a Spanish name comes up too – Sal Roca. Know him? What you got was also copied-in to this person. Checked him. Comes up harmless.' I thanked him and didn't ask how he got all the information. Maybe he was just computer savvy. So the sender was Hungarian. So was Liliane.

Ramon Masia emailed and asked if I would call him. I knew how Catalans had a dread of using the phone. He asked what day I was arriving with the group. 'A certain person wants to meet you. It is of interest for you.' It would be the owner of the altarpiece. I phoned him back and we agreed on the day and he said the meeting would be in his bookshop because it was private and he didn't want people overhearing what was said. I asked how many people would be at this meeting. Just one other.

'It will be of benefit for you.'

I asked if, by chance, he knew Roca?

'Yes. He worked for Dali and he is back in Girona.'

I asked what he was like.

'A very well-brought-up serious man, well travelled.' He hated being on the phone even if someone else was paying for it and hung up.

Why did Masia come out with the story now? I believed he had been surprised to get the photocopy. Did he now have the object in his shop? Was he given permission to make its existence known? The altarpiece photocopy did fit perfectly in the niche.

Peter Jack suggested our usual lunch and I was sure he'd produce the script. We gave our order and talked about Girona but I found I was not giving him as much as I used to. I was definitely not open. He did not mention the script so I supposed it would appear at the end of the meal. He would say, 'I have a surprise for you'. Or, 'The deals in the bag'. We got as far as his paying the bill so I had to ask to see the script.

'See it? I'm having some trouble there. I have to keep breaking off to do the bread-and-butter stuff. I think I'm being too loyal to the material and not getting my own voice.' He ordered another glass of red wine and continued with the problem. 'I just have to marry all the different lines of the story.'

'Why don't you get someone to do you a first draft? Just to have a base to work from?' I could see he was thinking.

'That's a cop-out. I really want to write it myself.'

'All this time?'

'Yeah, you must be getting pissed off with me.'

'I'll write it.'

'Well, you could.' He lifted the wine glass then saw it was emptied. 'But I'd feel bad if I didn't pay you and frankly right now with the schools and —'

'Minimum rates. I'll do it in a month.'

He did seem to think about it. 'Let me think about it. It's an idea.'

The next day he phoned as I was climbing stairs in the sudden heat, not at my best. He sounded edgy.

'I paid the money and I've got a whole year left till the end of the option. I've bought the time. It's mine.'

I wanted to scream: well get on with it!

I rang him right back. 'Some people might think the society got to you and bought you off. Well, you did make that trip all alone after meeting 3 Piece so they're paying to block the script. That's rich.' I hung up. No more contact with Peter Jack.

Then my agent said he was doing a mega TV series in the autumn. No bread-and-butter work here.

I took a last look at the photo before leaving for the Ryanair flight to Girona. The scene depressed me. It was too plain. Not starry enough. Flowers far too big.

16

Anna and I were in the wrong room. It was a reversal of the one we usually occupied and we both felt completely disorientated. The beds were the wrong way round and I mistook the bathroom for a cupboard, tripped over a previously unknown step, couldn't find the light switch. The mirrors made it worse and presented another reality altogether. Anna did slightly better than me but felt she was becoming stressed and had to get out. The man who called my room had good clear English and said his name was Roca. 'So, you know where to find me?' I said.

'Let's meet. I have things to tell you.'

I said I would see him downstairs.

'No, no. In the gardens of La Mercè and don't mention this to anyone. We must speak privately.'

And also speak less privately about his connection with a woman in Hungary who sent out photos that seem to be without point with a message that certainly had a point?

Before meeting him I found Miguel coming out of the kitchen and asked him about Roca. I also had more questions about the society. Did it have rituals that allowed an adept to cross into other spheres? Did it really exist? Miguel told me to ask de Puig.

Lluis Maria de Puig, the historian and politician, Spanish representative at the EU, had helped me with my research on *City of Secrets*. He was born in Girona right under the tower of the French woman's house but didn't remember it or her. 'A foreign woman living here alone at this time? Impossible. This is a funny place. Everything disappears.'

Liliane had had the answer. Rennes-le-Château is the north, Girona the south, Canigou the centre point. They form a golden mean. The south always disappears, the north remains, so Rennes still stands. Of course, Lluis Maria de Puig knew about the society and had given me two books by Carles Rahola, a journalist and unique force in Girona in the first half of the twentieth century. Imprisoned for his views, he had been murdered by Franco in 1925. 'These books are quite simply telling us about Girona,' de Puig had said. 'They give a good description of life here at that time. Nothing interesting for you really, except the title. Why does Rahola call this "The Tree of Life"? It's mystified many of us. Inside, the last page is the number 310.'

How wrong the politician turned out to be about these books. Coded, they told an underlying story concerning sites in the province.

On the Portal journey I had decided one thing regarding the society: maybe it wasn't trying to shut me up, but instead, see what I was doing and what I found. It had occurred to me in the vicinity of that mountain that I might know what they did not.

I went to meet Roca and when I arrived, the Mercè gardens seemed empty. He got up from behind the fountain. He had amazing blue eyes, and an exceptional face. He took my hand and I felt immediately easy with him. He had spent years with Dali and was possibly 41.

'Tomorrow you are going to be offered something that will please you. 4pm. Bookshop,' he said.

'Are you a postbox for a Hungarian woman who sends seemingly pointless photographs?' I replied.

'Not any Hungarian woman. She happens to be a Hapsburg like your guide, Liliane. I don't surprise you, surely? The society was made up of Hapsburgs at one time.' He continued as though not changing the subject. 'I've always admired José.'

'I just asked about the message. "Look at this, well."'

'To get your attention.'

'What's the purpose?'

'You tell me.'

He put a hand up to cover his eyes. He said he had trouble hiding his expressions. 'I saw José in the street. I introduced myself and mentioned your name. I hope you don't mind. He is an old man now, but beautiful.'

Oh God, not another in love with my lover? How many hadn't I heard say this? 'Married.'

'Of course, I know his story.' He put my book *City of Secrets* on the table. 'Sign it for me, please.'

I signed.

'Tomorrow is a new life for you. Please be there on time.' And we happened to be looking at each other and started laughing.

'So tomorrow is the first day of the rest of my life.'

'Or the last?'

The laughter came to an end and I could see the group, by chance, coming this way into the garden.

'We are hopeless,' he said. 'I am young. You are not. I am gay. You're a grandmother. I am rich. You are not. You have had some amazing things in your life. I might expect that in my future. You had José. But we love each other. It is terrible.'

And we laughed again and I said 'It's all right, you're Bambi.' He seemed to like that.

After he'd left I phoned José. But he wasn't there, not any of the hours I called. I met Luis in the street. 'How strange,' he said. 'I thought of you because I just saw José being helped onto a train for Paris.'

He seemed to be friendly enough but I remembered Filip's cautionary words. Did he work for the society? He asked if I was still doing tours. Later I discovered I needed people. They protected me from something that was dark. It was not the Portal.

I printed an A4 copy of the clip from Budapest. It slid out of the tray and lay the wrong way up and I was no longer looking at a glass table with four legs, a vase of flowers, a woman in a cocktail dress standing, back to camera. What I had in front of me was an oriental figure in a dress made of flowers carrying a crescent moon, like a baby in her arms. She wore a tall hat with a circle of light on the top and four sticks rising out of it. The figure had slanting eyes. I could make out the feet and thought it was female. Turning it round, I could see the vase, the glass table with four spindly legs, which made up the hat or headdress and the face. The bouquet did the rest. It produced a skirt or robe, two curving stalks made arms that cradled a long pale bloom lying sideways and made the shape of a crescent moon. The eyes were produced by two pieces of dark twig hanging down the top of the vase. Spin it around again and I thought the moon could be a baby. There was a small ball, which made a head.

Turning it right way up I saw the head was a bud. The way the figure held it, just centre, in bent arms over her midriff, made it more likely to be a baby. The way she held it was noticeable: quite confident, no fear, just holding it there in front of her. The hat was more a ceremonial headdress. The eyes caught the attention. I had never seen a figure like this one and the style of what she wore and how she stood, meant nothing to me. I was sure it was from a long time past.

The reversed woman in the hotel became a boat reflected in water: the legs — two masts, the shoes — the flags. Her skirt made up the boat, the rest was a reflection on water. I had never seen a boat like that, either. It made me think of the satanic windows. How it was possible to go on seeing something, which on closer view, was another thing altogether. And I felt this hotel room was only the skin of reality, reachable by a simple reverse.

So the oriental figure held a baby or crescent moon and had come from a boat all from a different time.

It's about reversal. Mirrors. The oriental figure with the baby and a boat wasn't as worrying as the hotel room and those flowers. I decided not to tell Lew Doyle.

17

I left the group in the hotel saying I'd be an hour and walked along to the bridge. Ramon Masia had left a message to say the meeting would be at a different venue and I would be met near his bookshop. I supposed we would go to the Arc bar. Anna and a local boy who played guitar were suddenly ahead of me on the clanking bridge and I could hear him cry, 'This is the last day of the rest of my life.' I had said that yesterday. Anna made a reply, which he did not accept.

'I have made my decision. I cannot let anyone else down.'

'But if you do that you are letting yourself down,' she promised him.

I wished they would hurry on and even when they were in the Rambla, out of sight, I could still hear their voices. The boy, a dropout from university, had joined our meditation group that morning unexpectedly and sang us his story accompanied by guitar. He would have taken over the whole event with his indecision to live or otherwise. Anna offered him some help. He obviously was in need of support and could not wait for their second session. By chance, they circled around my heavy journey in the heat towards the Calle Forsa. Then they were gone and I took a shortcut through the alley where the old hotel had been and I again heard their voices and they reappeared higher up.

'You have helped me but I am beyond living.' Sound of their climbing a flight of steps and I waited to be free of them. 'I have made the decision.' And back they came, lower down, crossing a narrow street and through to the river. 'I thought of going out to sea but you don't just get rid of yourself by dying. I am—so high—'

She was walking fast to keep up with him with her clean, neat, little walk and he came down from whatever high it was.

'I am in trouble and I don't know it.'

And I couldn't hear any more. The clamour of bells ringing the hour drowned all else. And then the birds started up. The sound of birds would be a sign of danger. At 16 after hitchhiking with Beryl to Seville we ended up in a Gypsy village nearby where I had been taken into the care of the grandmother. She told me I was 'La Savia' —'The one who knows'. I just needed to learn (or was it to relearn) the signs of divination. Certain bird cries could be a strong warning of danger.

Their formation in flight a potent of bad to come. The world, she said, would teach me everything if I knew how to read it. I remembered one thing—the message of the birds. It had once saved my life.

The men waited at the top of the Calle Forsa which was silent in this deserted siesta hour and each stood separate, unmoving and for a moment I felt I was going towards a sacrifice or some retribution. Was it the way the light fell that made their appearance unnerving? Closer now, I could see their expressions were too hard for what was simply a meeting that was going to offer me something to my advantage.

Then I recognized Ramon Masia and the young, sylph Roca whom I'd met only yesterday, yet he seemed not to know me and the other I did not know at first, yet he was not unfamiliar. The heat was tricky and kept me at a disadvantage. They were in a hurry and after a brief greeting walked me swiftly up a side street that for all my time in this city I did not recognize and helped me down through a low doorway into a darkened, deep-vaulted stone room. There seemed to be no choice about it and their behaviour was swift and decided and if I hadn't known of this meeting I would have thought it was a kidnap. The powerful one took a seat behind a table in the gloom and I thought his manner was familiar. The hair was different but I had seen him only briefly on two very different occasions. This was Gyp, the apparent guardian of the city who no one could identify, a man José described as 'not without a certain danger'.

The walls, now visible, were covered with projected images, circling slowly, some huge as posters and all of me. Sounds began, disquieting, too loud until it was not possible for me to hold this level of volume and behind me, figures slipped through the gloom, drawing close, making no noise; grey, nondescript people, all of them men. As the sounds increased more photographs flicked on, ever more going into my past. Whoever had done this, knew me inside and out: my wedding day, my children, the modelling days, the Hollywood years, my drama school productions, my bohemian days, the press releases and José. My life came towards me on waves of sound, a terrible intrusion, trying to break me down. Gyp sat still, much as he had on the day of the deluge in the Café Antigua and was covered in differing lights and pieces of my reflected life and all I had come here for was an opportunity that would please me. Where was Roca exactly? I looked behind me, quite horrified by the increasing number of these shadowy men still arriving from all sides.

Smaller, grainy photos now, enlarged from snapshots, private and personal, going back through the early years and some I didn't know and wondered how he could have obtained these. I said this was terrible. But any sound was drowned by the ever-increasing noise and the chilled dark filled up with waif-like figures, 30 or 40 men, I was sure I did not know. The street door was closed.

Gyp didn't have to do anything to claim my attention. 'You've worked hard for your age,' he told me.

In spite of my seemingly unenviable position, I was still young enough to dislike that remark. It occurred to me I could just get up and leave but something about this man kept me attentive as though this was the response he needed to obtain.

'You look for the secret. Some of this you have. We will give you the secret,' He spoke in French. His voice was strong and rich as a preacher's and rose above the hellish noise. 'No one in this city has ever thanked you for the work you have done. Most don't even know you. You are unsung. But we will show our gratitude. You will be offered what will please you because you deserve it.' His voice and the sound from the walls jarred together into something that even for me was beyond acceptable.

I bent forward and covered my ears and the photographs pushed their way, more than ever, into my consciousness, my whole life a punishment, the sounds arranged in hypnotic order to break down all resistance.

'You will be offered the role necessary to be shown the secret. And then you will be initiated and remain here in this city.' His voice was too deep, too discordant. 'Come and see what we offer you.' He opened his arms generously. 'All is yours. Just climb the stairs with us.' He rose from his chair.

That was where they would do it. And it would look like an accident.

'All this is yours: the house, the land, the gardens. Your expenses paid. You are the chosen one, next in the custodial line. And the last. You are the last. You have the secret.' He waited for me to be grateful.

My legs were shaking and I hoped my heart would be on my side and stand up to what came next. Its beating was the flutter of a trapped bird. And the men crowded closer, not quite flesh and blood, wrapped in a grey mist.

And I had the one last thought that might save me. José! 'What does he say about this?'

Gyp gestured with his hands, a full, satisfying indication of doom. 'José. He is finished.'

He was coming towards me but didn't touch me. Could I just run around the men to the heavy door and into the unknown street, which had been surely uncovered for this private occasion, as if by medieval ritual? I could see the mention of José would buy me nothing in here. God would be a better ally.

'What's the matter with her?' asked the man behind me.

'She hasn't come round to it yet,' Gyp was impatient. 'She still thinks she has choice.'

And the years I'd passed through, with a fair share of pain and adversity, were surely good for something. I straightened up and looked at this rich-voiced captor. 'José won't like this. You'll have to answer to him. And we'll see who has choice. He won't forgive you for this.'

And I wasn't sure of my territory as far as José was concerned, of what, if anything, he would do to save or avenge me. And my body started to swirl around with the many circling versions of me at all ages and my heartbeat was lost in the threatening drumming from the stone room and my life seemed very short.

'Be wise now and follow what is offered.'

He still held out his hand to help me from the chair. 'You are the most disobedient of all.' The photographs were circling madly like a fairground ride gone wrong and the sounds stuck in an atonal chord.

I thought I said, 'My money's on José.'

'José's gone. We've put him on a train for Paris.' Dismissive, then, of José.

'You won't win,' I promised.

He tried again to take my hand and lead me away. 'I think you should see what I offer you.' The men waited, a little restless now. Was their leader going to let them down? Gyp sighed and moved papers on the table. 'The trouble is, you will stay.' His voice was quiet, just for him and me. The atonal stuck sound fading, images running into each other, all upturned and rolling down from all ages, like some multiple road accident.

'Stay? Oh, I don't think so,' I said. He did seem surprised. 'I'll go away.' And straightened up, ready to leave.

'Away?' he echoed. 'Where?' He was definitely surprised. 'How?'

'I'll just go.' And it was almost time for me to get up from the chair.

'But there's nowhere to go.' He paused, almost sad. 'You're in it and it's in you.' The men watched as Gyp approached his disobedient, ungrateful recipient. Gently he helped me up from the chair. 'Just come and see what waits for you and this bad moment will be forgotten.' He held me and the door seemed a long way off. I stared into the alarmed eyes of Ramon Masia and would have spoken but he made sure he looked away. Gyp, with gentle force, moved me to a flight of stone steps and talking all the while encouraged me to the first floor. It opened onto a patio on which a stone figure held a crescent moon, or was it a baby? The eyes were slanted. Gyp stood beside me and spoke not without love, 'She is beautiful but what she carries more so and it is still here.'

And in that moment I knew I would never be free.

18

I did not expect to walk away from Gyp and I suppose at one moment or another, someone would, all of a sudden, be there changing my supposed plans for the evening. Gyp would want me returned. At one point as he'd introduced the courtyards, the salons, the gardens of this unknown territory he did say I could be shown the secret at any moment I chose. I could see he was stirred up by my numb reaction.

'The secret is the journey.'

Was he talking about the eleven sites of the passage I'd taken with Lil?

The exit from this property was directly onto the maze of cobbled alleys and stairways at the apex of the old quarter and we faced the statue of the Madonna with the Pear at a cross-point above a fountain. Gyp gave an account of how the pear had perplexed the inhabitants since the statue had been placed there in the sixteenth century.

His French was efficient and these Catalan men, whether they understood or not, listened obediently and while he was so occupied I slipped away down the flight of stairs behind me keeping to the shaded wall, one step after another and each one was an act of freedom I certainly did not expect. I judged I was out of sight and no one came after me. And then I realized Gyp had let go of my hand to point out the pear on the right-hand side of the woman and someone like Gyp would never let go of anyone, especially someone he held captive unless he no longer had any use of them. I'd got away because he'd let me, for now. The bookshop was closed but I was sure I saw Masia and the daughter watching me from the partly closed shutters. I reached the nearest public place, the Arc bar, and just sat outside, waiting to recover. I sat for a while before I could phone Cynthia and hearing the way I sounded she lost no time getting to the bar and I realized in spite of the drama, which she certainly anticipated, she was also concerned. In full throttle she arrived, hair flapping up and down wildly, cheeks on fire, legs stretching with a strength they did not have in shoes that would disintegrate, her feet with them, within the hour. She sat quite collapsed for a few moments and then ordered tea.

For me there were no words, no explanation. I must just stay in the practical, earthly moments waiting for the afternoon's events to become manageable. There was before and after. Cynthia belonged to the before.

'You've had a psychic shock,' she decided, and a tired pudding, not a million miles away from a lemon sorbet, caught her eye and she spooned it up quickly, 'To keep going.'

All I knew was that I was outside the Arc bar and I felt estranged from my usual self and hoped by sitting calmly I would recover. They had simply let me leave. Had they? I told her what I could and realized I could never tell it as it had been. Verbal recollection could not make sense of that happening. She was impressed enough to say, 'This is what you have always been prepared for. I always felt your journey through Girona was spiritually meant.'

I was surprised to hear this.

'It makes sense your coming here as you did, at 15, and meeting José and never being free of this place or that man. So there is a purpose — it is for you to be custodian. It would seem something you have already prepared yourself for.' And she mentioned the psychic work, the healing, the writing, the making sense of what otherwise would be uncovered or, at most, mysterious. 'You and José were meant to meet. I've always had that impression.'

She was holding my hand and said I should think calmly about what the man had offered. There was no need to be upset. She could see I was very upset. She said they had obviously displaced José and taken over.

The problem was I did feel even more displaced than my old lover. The slant-eyed figure carrying the crescent moon or baby had not done me any good at all. Cynthia liked practical solutions.

Out of something bad could come something good and tangible. There had been too many divorces (parents, friends), and soon, her own.

'You will get all this property and money and possibly power and it can't just be sniffed at. What has José ever given you? We are not getting any younger. Let's have a quiet dinner alone and decide what to say. How have you left it with them?'

I hadn't. I did remember Sal Roca had looked at me with fury. 'You have let him know somehow we know each other. He is now my enemy because he knows I disobeyed him and met you before I should. I was only trying to help.' And he'd walked away desolate.

Cynthia said, 'Do you want me to take over the talk this evening?'

What was the way out? To be ahead of the game.

I couldn't face the group, took the stairs to the room and did the usual things; the shower, the exercises, the drinking water with lemon. It all seemed superfluous. I hoped it was just shock and the best answer was to continue with the group.

Gyp was a man used to control, getting his way; a military or police past, and the 40 men around had watched and waited for his next order or decision. He had conviction. He spoke, he did not listen. What did he want? Acquiescent action.

Who was Gyp?

Why was I even suitable as a custodian or was it shepherdess? Why did this man want me? Was it something I knew and should not know? Something I'd heard and should not hear? Suddenly I couldn't think at all. Everything had just stopped. Had he known my guide Liliane? So few knew him and he seemed to pass through Girona invisibly. I thought of the number five, in Masia's bookshop that magicians used. How could he not just appear but seem different on each occasion? The man in the Antigua was not as tall as the one who'd waited patiently with the photographs outside the Arc bar. What did he see in me that he could use? Was I really the one formed to be the next and last custodian of the society? If they'd wanted something from me they couldn't have gone about it more unsuccessfully. I was frightened to death.

When I joined the group for dinner I was ready to talk about the two altarpieces and the two towers and I did not venture into the affairs of the afternoon and Cynthia said I was doing all right. The next day we would go to Rennes and see the altarpiece there. I did get the sense the group was aware something unexpected had happened. Their eyes looking at me were curious. I expected Cynthia had covered my long absence with some part of this revelatory news. I said the coach would come around 10.30 the following morning and went to my room.

The reversed room was now the only thing that made sense. I was on the other side of a matching landscape. What was left in here was right out there. The mirror in here duplicated the one on the other side of the wall in the reversed room next door but at an angle. The lamp formed another. The two rooms made a matching territory that in me no longer caused confusion. I seemed to fit into this dual condition. It had a mathematical precision that calmed me. I woke in the night and clearly saw what had most upset me: the statue of the slant-eyed woman carrying the crescent moon baby.

The next morning the receptionist said no one had called, and I was surprised. I confirmed the coach for Rennes-le-Château. It had leaked out to the group that something out of the ordinary had happened, and they seemed excited and ready for the next surprise and in no hurry to leave all this for Rennes-le-Château. Apparently Sal Roca had turned up in the night, upset, needing to see me. It seemed I could be in a bad situation and should leave and he would take me to the border. Cynthia had tried to take care of him. It was 2 a.m. but he'd rushed off into the night and I asked why she hadn't called me.

'You needed your rest.' She needed her drama.

Now this morning he was back, a little careworn but ready for normal action. It was 10 a.m. and he walked into the breakfast room accompanied by Gyp and Masia, all made-up and friends again, even smiling. Gyp clapped his hands, 'Off we go!' He meant me. I explained my group and I were going to France.

'Oh, I have something much better.'

98

The group stared at him, variously liking him, admiring him, intrigued. I couldn't but not see Roca's eyes as they searched mine, pleading, beseeching, do what he says!

'But I have this group, Gyp.' I stood up and tried to encourage him back into the foyer. He would not be encouraged. 'I have to go with them.'

'You want them? They can come. Let's go.'

Everything happened quickly, nothing quicker than the group's members plunging into the vehicles lined up by the door. A flick of his fingers and the coach was cancelled. His group of men squeezed into the Land Rover. Sal Roca would translate and half sat on Cynthia's lap. The convoy sped out of Girona.

'What is the something better, Gyp?' I asked. Masia and another man laughed.

'They have made a nice effort to patch up,' I said to Cynthia and then I remembered Gyp might speak English.

19

It was Gyp's show from the start and I should have seen it. He had us all in his charge and he orchestrated the day, handing out material and information like a captain preparing for battle. His military base was the restaurant, Can Bosch, outside Dali's castle at Pubol, where he described quickly the journey, trod not only by current initiates but Saunière, Cocteau, Otto Rahn, Dali and his wife, Gala. It seemed fortuitous that both Dali's last chef and driver were in the vicinity of the restaurant as Gyp spoke. It was not quite as it seemed as Gyp had set them up in advance, to be there at a particular time to meet me, the, as he described, 'well-known visitor to Dali's house in earlier times'. I was the ace, they the confused. They nodded in the right places and in Catalan explained a little of what they'd done for the great artist. Roca did a good job with the translation. Gyp signalled 'enough', hugged them as though they were relatives and told them to go off and have a drink.

It was about this time that the photographer buzzed around us like an indefatigable insect and not one nebulous detail passed that he did not capture. I waited for Gyp to get rid of him. Not a chance. Gyp had brought him. Gyp told my group of eight that they had come so far in my care but now, in his, would reap the reward. He spoke some Spanish, mostly Catalan, all translated by Roca. To me he spoke only French. Each time I edgily started to reclaim my role with the group, he changed the subject and spoke in a respectful manner, referring to me as the custodian, the shepherdess, the last in the line. He told them I would hold the secret, conduct the ritual, tread the path of the sages before me. I was the one who would 'know'. La Savia. And I remembered my early journey to the south of Spain and the Gypsy grandmother's teachings. Had he got hold of this too? It all sounded sincere and good, and Cynthia nudged me. 'This is where they will do it.' She pointed to the castle 'make you the custodian'.

I needed preparation and answers. It seemed he was bringing our consciousness to another point, which he held and I could receive. He spoke of Saunière as an old friend. No mention of José. Gyp was not prepared to be a listener and told us what he needed us to know, his manner swift and to the point. He said I had been formed to take the role given to me and it was no mistake that I had been so drawn to Girona. It was no love affair or illusion that had brought me back, time and time again, to this place. My life and the pain I had gone through, the qualities I'd been given before birth, the hard work I'd endured, prepared me for this role, which was a gift from spirit. I felt now as Cynthia did that this role would be suddenly, publicly, offered and there would be little time for discussion. He quickly turned to the growing pile of freshly photocopied papers Ramon Masia was placing before him and took the first three sheets. 'This is the secret.' He held them up and I wondered why it was always three. They were covered with sacred geometry. 'The key will be the property of the shepherdess.'

'The secret is not gold, or treasure. It is the journey and it is made up of two matching territories, one to the north and Girona in the south. They are duplicated. What is historically man-made and the landscape both mirrored, one place to another.' Quickly he handed round a sheet to each of us. 'This is what everyone has been looking for.'

It was a map created by Boudet, of the Rennes-le-Château area which when reversed became part of the Girona landscape.

'The Valley of San Daniel. You all know it,' he said

They did not. Black mark for me. I quickly told them it was beneath the Barraca site.

He waited impatiently. 'You have a tomb here, a church, a tower, a track crossing a river. That's Girona. Turn it. Rennes. Saunière knew the secret, this is why he came here. There is much more for you to discover.' He spoke firmly and simply with power. 'Next. The Madonna with a child and a pear.' Masia tried to be quick, handing the sheet to the group. 'And now the key.' He lifted a copy but there were none for us. 'On it you will see three things. What are they? They are the locations. This afternoon we will turn the key.'

I cut in, also firmly, 'This afternoon we have other things to do. We are going to examine the altarpiece here and in Rennes.'

He looked up almost sorry for me. 'But it is here.'

'Yes, and in Rennes.'

He shook his head. 'I will show you the true altarpiece. You and your group will see it tomorrow.'

I told him we had other plans. He didn't even listen.

The group tried not to look in my direction. I chose my best answer, the only one I had. 'The group and I will discuss it.'

I knew which way the group would go and so did he. I could see Cynthia wanted a visit to the ladies' room but would go through any ignobility before leaving this exchange. Not without respect, each one held the photographed sheets as though they gave the secret of the universe.

He spoke softly. 'They never stop looking but without result. It is here.' He stabbed a thumb downwards towards the ground. 'This is why two thousand years ago the Magdalene came here.'

There was a general stirring, a sense of surprise. 'She, the shepherdess,' he pointed to me, 'will be shown the route they took, what they found and what we still have here today.'

He slapped his pages back in the folder and the group didn't know whether to applaud.

Back in his car, with several of the men, he leaned out to me. 'Roca is taking you around the castle. I'll see you here at five.'

Yes, Gyp had set up a very nice dynamic: he and I, the holder and the recipient, the leader and the participant, the priest and the goddess. The list would go on.

He had succeeded in diverting my group and made sure they would follow his trail. Why did he want them? The answer crept slowly through the heat into my brain. To keep me here. They had paid the tour and I would stay for the duration. One of the women, her eyes bright, exclaimed, 'This is the greatest secret of two thousand years.' Her eyes were now dangerously bright. 'This is the society.'

Yes, maybe, but was he from the society? I was as ready to be impressed as the next person and as we sat down to a good lunch in the shade I didn't know anymore if I was a writer recording my journey of discovery or the chosen one, the shepherdess, the person of many names. Roca, I noticed, stayed away with the Catalan owners and he did not look pleased. Masia, when asked questions, knew less French than when he was trying to sell postcards. His words disappeared into a prudent silence as he ate with pleasure the copious meal. The photographer relentlessly recorded our eating habits and I asked him to stop. Cynthia tried to get my attention and I gave her my Catalan flan, cousin of the mousse, and indicated we sit alone under a tree.

'Does he own the property he wants to give to you?' She was always good on property. 'It's probably belonging to the society. Is it his to give?' The others settled beside us. 'I don't like him,' she whispered.

I decided I would ask him to explain the custodial role he had offered me and give him an answer when I'd spoken to José.

The group were excited. It couldn't get any more spontaneous and thrilling. It sure wasn't a repeat of endless flyblown tours already exhausted by repetition. What they wanted to know was: what I would do? Second: who was Gyp?

I caught Roca on his own and asked what was going on and his eyes flicked sideways indicating Masia, who had joined us, silent, smiling, the smile filling his plump face like that of the Cheshire cat. He asked if I was happy. 'Gyp brings good things, no?'

Back to Roca and my mouth opened and his eyes, glacial, pleaded for silence. 'We have to take the group around the castle,' he said quickly. 'Gyp wants them to understand Dali's significance in this discovery.'

He knew his material and took us through what had been Gala's home and grounds until her death in 1982. And then Dali had moved there as though to be near her memory. Roca brought her to life as we moved through the salons and boudoirs and he talked of her rituals, her influence, her lovers, and we were introduced to: the significance of the figures, the signs, the shapes, psychic journeys, the artworks, the thin elephants, the extraordinary giraffes. He explained the point of the colours, how they all played a part intensifying her life. I assumed Dali had created most of this for her. This Russian muse had lived with Max Ernst, the poet Paul Éluard and then married Dali. Roca knew her nature and brought it into focus for us. Was she a member of the society? Without doubt, Roca assured me. A photograph on the stairway going up to the bedroom, taken late in life, showed a young, obviously sexual, boy playing the piano. He was full of himself and his recent conquest, not one musically. And she was huddled against the wall on the floor shrivelled with a reptilian smile, her eyes gleaming, proud. She had enjoyed the pianist, and later the music, the conquest was not all his.

'That's a wig,' said Cynthia. 'Doesn't suit her.'

Roca couldn't wait to defend the diva. 'She needed men. Had to have them around the clock.'

The women did not like Gala. Roca changed the subject abruptly and explained the significance of the decoration and furnishing of each chamber, and through this, a celebration of opulence, I could sense a shrill, endless, high-pitched cry passing through the castle, unceasing. It was pain. 'He must have suffered,' I said.

'Who? Gyp?' said Cynthia.

'Dali.'

Not for Roca, who in turn, celebrated the artificial. 'The objects have attracted other energies and that is their purpose.' And to me he added, 'Dali understood her and what she found necessary.' He turned and faced a dress, hanging beside the photograph. 'This is the red Chanel dress she was buried in.'

'Surely a copy,' said Cynthia. But Roca was out swiftly and onto the road to be in time for Gyp Planas's return.

At exactly five o'clock Gyp drove up with a new set of men, some carrying ropes, saws, torches. He told us to be quick and opened the car door so I could sit beside him. I asked where we were going. 'To la Pera, the pear, the fruit of the Madonna.' My group were not quick enough, did not scramble into the cars and he shouted to Roca to stop them talking and place them in whatever vehicles had space and, turning his car, he sped out of the village.

He did everything in too much of a hurry. Did he have permission for any of this? Cynthia's question, 'Who owned the properties?' needed consideration. I couldn't tell at this point who owned what. Did Gyp own this information he was giving out so freely? What role did he play, if any, in the society? He drove across superb countryside known with good reason as the Golden Triangle and after ten minutes came to a shuddering stop, in a hamlet with a church and little else. 'This tenth-century church houses the Lady with the Pear.' He gathered our group inside and his men waited outside. I asked why they needed the equipment. Were they going to scale the wall to the steeple?

'No. They're going to hack a path up a hill so you and your group can reach a most privileged place.'

I had noticed the torches. 'In the dark?' I asked.

'If necessary.'

I was positioned beneath the Madonna for endless photographs.

'So what does the pear mean?' he asked the group.

'The womb,' suggested Piers Ainsworth, a Cambridge graduate, he seemingly the most knowledgeable.

'The fruit of the womb. So who is she?' Was he pointing at me or the statue?

'The Magdalene, obviously,' said Piers.

Cynthia cut in, 'The pear represents descendants.'

'Exactly.' Gyp turned to where she sat, giving her attention for the first time.

'The Magdalene usually wears red,' Piers spoke again. She wasn't this time. Red was back there in the castle with the Chanel dress. Her robe was pale-peach, draped with a blue wrap.

The church was enclosed and airless and Gyp led us to a narrow flight of curving stairs. Three of the women were outsize or more, how were they supposed to climb here? Ramon Masia's stomach only just passed the opening. Amazingly, everyone else in the group got up these ever narrowing flights to the first level. 'People must have been smaller and shorter when these were built,' said Roca. The stairs were dotted with rat poison, disintegrating rats and traces of cement dust.

Cynthia sat in the tenth-century window, sweat dripping freely, threatening her newly curled hair. She kicked off her shoes.

'There's another flight to the top and then you see the view.' Roca asked who, if anyone, would go up. He was not unaware of the heavier ladies. They would all go up. Thin as a wand, Roca had no trouble speeding up ever tightening curving flights of claustrophobic hell. Apart from Masia I was the only one not up for this. I hoped my unwillingness would not go against any custodial role in the future but I needed to negotiate my way down. I became wedged between one unrelenting wall and the next and the spiral tightened, the steps narrowed. Behind me Masia, now trapped by my inability to move, gave instructions, any one of them enough to finish me up in paramedics' care. Panic not far away I could hear Roca translating an account of the church and Perillos in France and between the two, what he called, a direct line of control.

I called to him to help me and he brought both Masia and me down slowly, skilfully. 'Don't look, just step. Hold the walls.'

Never again! I was angry with Gyp. How could he let us be so vulnerable, at risk, people he didn't know and hadn't questioned as to their climbing skills, vertigo, claustrophobia, rats—dead or alive—phobias? Once down, I sat on the nearest seat and stared reproachfully at the Lady with the Pear. 'It is known,' said Roca softly, 'the Magdalene is associated with this fruit. They have named a pear after her.' I got up and opened the church door and breathed fresh air. How would the large ones get down? I had learned something else about Gyp. He had seemed responsible. He was not responsible. Masia, having done the last deceptively difficult flight on his own, was still panting, face highly coloured. I told him to come to the doorway and breathe. He considered going straight out for a brandy. The photographer came down next, flapping his face. He hadn't liked it either. I waited for the others, the calamity which would surely come. Thankfully, I had insisted they take their own insurance.

The British actor, still jetlagged from his LA flight was descending backwards on all fours. At the bottom he smacked the dust off his hands and held onto a prayer book. ' I could have done without this. Trapped up there where claustrophobia meets vertigo, suffocation and stupidity.'

'You mean Gyp?'

'Myself, for being there.' He cleaned his hands in the water stoup. 'You certainly meet the edge on this trip.' And then he asked how I was doing and I said a little strange and I realized since being in yesterday's happening with Gyp, nothing was the same. It was as though I was no longer in myself but slightly out to one side. My consciousness was not quite attached. I, too, put my hands in the stoup and the actor put his hands on my forehead and made the sign of the cross. He looked at me gravely as though he did not like what he saw. I thought then I should go to a priest.

'If you're in it, you're in it,' said the actor, answering me although I had not spoken.

The sound of steps, sure and orderly, as the group got themselves down uncomplaining, glad they'd seen what they had.

'This is also a Templar site,' Gyp said. 'My family for generations have come from there.'

Was this the old family that had held the altarpiece from the French woman's house? I asked who his family were exactly.

'We go back many centuries to the crusades.'

I could see Roca, as he translated the words, was strained, his face tight, mouth dry, eyes restless. 'The Magdalene with the symbol of fertility is depicted in several sites here and just across the border in France. She carries the pear to show she carried the child. Some statues show her with three. They are the descendants.'

Piers Ainsworth, eyes closed, with the magnificence of it all, said he'd come on a simple speculative tour and was now holding the secret of two thousand years.

'Descendants of who, exactly?' said the actor.

Gyp paused and then allowed two words 'the key'. Another pause. He wasn't afraid of pauses when they were his own. 'This opens the way. Which in turn opens our understanding. Some of this was given to me, the rest I worked out for myself. We will unlock this material tomorrow. Ten o'clock.' He held up his hand. Did they agree?

They did. He got into the car and the other door was held open, presumably for the shepherdess. I said I'd rather go with Roca.

'For all our sakes go with him.' And Roca encouraged me into the vehicle and closed the door. Yes, his tan was more obvious and there was pale, shocked flesh underneath. I noticed Gyp look at him. Just one look, assessing.

Gyp drove fast and the others did what they could to follow. I expected to hear something more of yesterday's custodial role offer but he talked non-stop about the key, how much time it had taken, how it would affect the way we saw history.

I asked about José.

'Finished. He is an old man. He says one thing, does another.'

'Didn't seem that way in the Antigua cafe, that rainy day.'

'Forget José. You will be the key to the future,' he told me. 'You work here and carry the story, hold the role.'

'Who do you answer to?' I asked him.

He asked what exactly I meant.

'Who directs you?'

He allowed a smile. 'You are not ready for that.'

'So, when am I the custodian?'

'You already are.' It was a day of surprises.

So there we had it: the custodian and the controller. He would get me doing what he wanted, but I would know little about him. In Catalan he spoke to Masia and I understood he wanted Roca alone for a few minutes. Masia did not look happy. Gyp saw the car carrying the pale, tanned translator was overtaking us. 'He thinks he can slip away.' Cynthia used the conversation to give me advice. 'You are being used.' Gyp didn't react but his eyes flicked to the mirror so he caught any expression she might have. Did he or did he not speak English?

He dropped Cynthia at the hotel and waited for me to join her. I said I needed to talk to him. I said I wanted to see the territory I'd been offered. He answered his mobile. I still stayed where I was. He seemed to give up and reversed back into the main road and up the Calle Forsa. Being alone with Gyp was a surprise. There was suddenly nothing to say. Neither of us spoke. He drove around the cathedral, seemingly looking for something and stopped by the statue of the Madonna with the Pear. Now at the door of the hidden territory I wasn't as happy being alone with him. He gestured at the property then looked at his watch.

'I thought you wanted to talk to Roca,' I said. 'Are you worried you'll lose him?'

He half laughed. 'I can always find Roca. It would be hard for me to lose him.'

Then he looked at me directly, into my eyes, and it was a disturbing moment, like a *coup de foudre*, a falling in love, a chemical moment, a shock, a capture.

I looked away as though curious about the property. I was determined not to react or weaken by speaking or asking him questions. I wanted to know why he said I could never be free. I said, 'Where did you get the statue of the oriental female carrying the crescent moon or baby?'

'Where is this?'

'Where it was yesterday, on the patio.'

He did seem to be trying to recall the moment I was talking about. I helped him. 'At the top of the stairs.'

'No, nothing like that.'

I insisted to see it. I'd go in now, even alone.

'It was the heat. You were overcome.'

I knew when I would finally get in there the statue would be gone.

20

Luis at the Arc told me the same story about José going to Paris. I asked how he looked. 'Yes, he's good.'

Back in my room I phoned Masia and he answered laughing. 'We have adventures together. Those steps. You are slimmer than me. He is good, Gyp. Your group love him.' I got the feeling he wasn't alone.

I tried the custodian, Dr Arnau in Ripoll and rang the number that had worked in Masia's shop. It wasn't about Howard Hughes this time. Or maybe it was. Dr Arnau did not know Gyp. I described him. He knew him even less. What was I doing in Girona exactly? he asked. I said I'd been made an offer I did not understand. I would speak to José but he was supposedly in Paris. I said all this had made me — what word did justice? — 'distressed.' I concluded I needed advice. He was silent, enough for it to be meaningful. I was about to add that he, as the custodian of the society, could help me but if I had been offered that role then what exactly was he?

'What, exactly, are you offered?'

Not sure of anything now, I played it down and made it vague. I asked what was his role in the society? He didn't reply.

'So who is the custodian?' I asked.

Silence.

'José Tarres was.' His voice was gentle, almost calming and I asked if I could come and see him. He would call me back. I felt all this was new to him. I also felt if you can't leave the table, be ahead of the game.

A short tap on the door, Roca came quickly into the room.

'He got rid of me.' He sat on the bed. 'He uses sensors. Over-hears everything.'

'Is he in the police or military?'

'He's in something, to go around Girona just as he pleases and no one sees it. I only know he doesn't like it that I met you before his afternoon performance.'

I asked why the three of them had quarrelled.

'It went wrong. You didn't go for it. They need you, for now. Possibly to get rid of José.'

He was suddenly quiet and in the silence I realized everything had a strange vibration as though my ears were blocked or some electric device, switched on, was in the room. I went to the window, drank some water. 'Maybe the military want to take it over?' I said. 'Maybe it's political.' I covered the mirror. It was too bright. 'Why do they want me?' I made it sound casual.

'I think they want to find out what you know,' he said. 'They think you know it all. That José told you. Maybe you do but I have to hide out now. He's after me. I'll go to France.'

I wondered what, exactly, Gyp would do. 'Who does he work for?'

'I don't know. I've only just been brought into this.'

I said he should stay with me and running out wasn't the answer.

He got up and looked out of the window down at the street. 'I've been away from here too long. It's always been a city of secrets.'

He added that after Dali died he went on working at the castle and then left for New York and South America. He'd always been involved with 'The Mysteries,' an underlying reality. It was the only thing that made sense in the end.

Another look from the window and he decided it was okay to leave.

I wasn't happy to see him go. Suddenly I had many questions, starting with how dangerous is this? But he was gone, softly down the staff stairs.

I sat in the Mercè gardens with Cynthia and Anna. Perhaps not the best choice, it hadn't been too good for Roca.

'It must be money,' said Cynthia 'Gyp's been paid.'

'Or knowledge, or power,' I said.

'Neither,' said Anna.

'Knowledge and money bring power,' said Cynthia. 'He's brought you in suddenly. It's not as though you've had any time to think about it. I think we should confront him.'

'Confront him all you like, he won't tell you anything. He's trained in confrontation,' said Anna.

Cynthia wasn't pleased. 'He doesn't tell her enough. You can't just bring someone into this.'

'He's done nothing wrong,' said Anna. 'He offered her something. He thrilled the group. He's saved us having to drag across to Rennes-le-Château. When has José Tarres done anything lately? Let's see what Gyp has got to show her.'

Piers was quietly beside us. 'I agree,' he said. 'I was sitting over there and overheard.' He pointed beyond the fountain. 'This is really important stuff. What he's talking about people have been looking for for hundreds of years.'

'What is he talking about?' said Anna.

'Let's ask the group,' I stood up—if he had been behind the fountain they were probably not far off in the trees—'if they want to go on.'

'They do,' Piers assured me. 'He's a knowledgeable person, prepared to share. Obviously the society want this out now. He's good to you.' He meant me.

Good? When did that end and bad begin? Truthfully, I couldn't make Gyp out.

Lew Doyle was the last person I'd call but it was late into the night and I could not sleep. I had been taken out of myself that was it. I described it as best I could.

'But if they offer you the custodial role, take it,' he said.

'But the group—'

'Forget the group. Drop them. Take the role.' Completely cut and dried regarding the group.

He said he would come to Girona and check it all out. I bet he would.

112

The author and José Tarres, who has been the pulse of the province, defending its customs

Girona the Immortal City, where nothing much changes

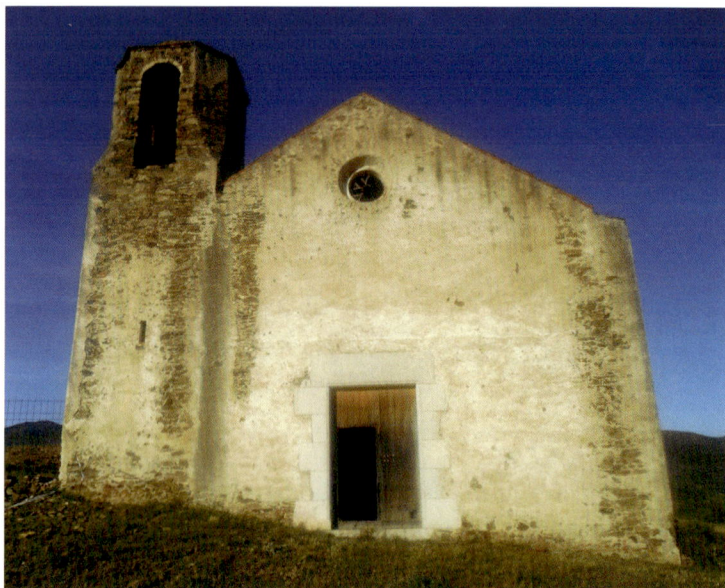

A little-known chapel in the region of the cradle site

Venus is the predominant influence on the cradle site. There are several temples in the area and this one has a vast view of the mediterranean coastline

The effigy of the oriental woman — in a small church in the mountains near the cradle site — has puzzled people for decades. What part did she play in Catholic ritual and Catalan culture?

Painting on wall of the hidden chapel. The symbolic cutting of the women's head is said to indicate the changing of thoughts

The author and lawyer, Kim. The Society is made up of mainly professional people with connections beyond the frontier

Author with a healing stone. It is said that the holes in the stone contained nutrients to restore and heal the sick

21

Early morning, Piers dared to phone at an ungodly hour to say they were there: Gyp, his men and three cars. Normally, I never set out before 10.00. I stepped onto the street my breakfast unfinished and Gyp said good morning in French and didn't look at me.

I waited for the group to be placed in the cars, then asked for Roca. Still not looking at me, Gyp said he was not there. I said we needed a translator but this was all arranged, it seemed. The woman from the US, Cathy, with her reasonable Spanish had said she would do it. Gyp stared at her, decided he liked her, but I still got the seat next to him. I asked if the group was happy to change direction. They were. This was bigger than anything expected and also they were in the vicinity of someone, me, who could be extolled, taken to other realities, be in real danger or go mad. This was better than digging out the provenance of two altarpieces.

For the next hours, he took us on a tour of 'the key'. Was this the key José had mentioned beyond price that I had held for a while and had unhappily mislaid? Gyp's sites, mainly stones and graves obedient to sacred geometry, were equidistant. A later site, the Benedictine monastery, I remembered from my early visits to the city. The Valley of San Daniel, adjoining the old part of Girona, had always been referred to as a mystery. The triangular shaped hill of Mount O was said to be exceptionally old and at its peak, centuries ago, existed a lunar church. I did remember a stone altar amongst the church remains, now long since gone. José used to refer to a burial place near the monastery, its secrets not even to be voiced aloud.

Gyp led us to this opposite side of the valley and pointed across the monastery to Mount O. He showed us these places on his latest photocopied map. 'Here you have the altarpiece you are looking for, all exactly 310 metres distance apart.'

'I hope he's right,' said the actor. 'Drawing these geometric patterns is uncertain. They could have used a thick pencil, then anything fits.'

'So, where exactly is the altarpiece?' I asked.

'Here.' He sounded reverent. 'This is the grave where the Magdalene sat daily in mourning for him and she prayed for his ascent.'

For a moment I thought he meant Jesus. Others in the group hoped he did. He meant Joseph of Aramathea.

'And the grave?'

'You're on it.'

He pointed a mere yard away to a mound covered with branches. Almost whispering, he described the altarpiece and pointed out aspects from the landscape in view.

One tower was missing these days, but everyone remembered that. 'They think the picture is a grotto in Rennes-le-Château. It is here.'

Piers got it immediately. 'It's made up of the landscape.'

'Exactly.' And Gyp pointed to the grave. 'She sat on the left and what do you see in front and behind her?' He tried to get me to recreate the position of the Magdalene and when I refused, Cathy was quick to oblige. Most of the men got it. They had been to the grotto near Rennes, where the Magdalene was supposed to have sat in mourning but curious features of the location had always worried them. Behind her, in the Rennes grotto, all three land-marks in the altarpiece were not visible. Here in Girona, they were. Gyp took my arm. 'And over there are the Stones.' He was pointing at Mount O. 'They mark what we have all been looking for. The graves of the descendants of the Magdalene.'

After an interval, allowing the group's outburst to die down, he pointed to a more accessible grave and started lifting the bracken. As though by magic, we were looking down into a narrow hole with a tunnel at a right angle which quickly went out of sight. 'That's where he is buried, Joseph of Aramathea.'

Anna laughed inappropriately. 'He had to make it with that one. He really wants to say Jesus.'

I looked down at history. The trouble, I wasn't good at graves.

At some point, Gyp dropped the term, 'Blue Apples'. I knew it was the last part of one of the coded parchments found in the church of Rennes-le-Château and ever since, hours have been spent trying to decipher them. Gyp had already done it.

The Blue Apples were the Stones on Mount O. Sixteen of them. They were sacred graves. Were they?

'So, they are the Magdalene's descendants?' asked our interpreter. Gyp nodded solemnly, waiting for the obvious question that would follow. She could barely say the word. In fact, I had never heard Jesus said like that. 'So that's what the society protects?' she concluded. Gyp nodded but his attention was on me. The shepherdess was getting a little restless. The descendants' story would not be one of my custodial priorities.

'Tired?' he asked.

Tired covered a lot of ground. It could even account for rebellious shepherdess' statements he now foresaw would follow. He did not want me undermining his position with the group or his men.

Back at the hotel, I called Masia and asked what had happened to Roca. He laughed long enough to think up an answer.

'He will always be all right, that boy. He comes from a wealthy, illustrious family in this city. You have no need to worry.' I asked him to get a message to Roca to contact me. I tried to ask about Gyp but he said he was suddenly busy with clients.

Of course, I should have gone to Miguel.

Miguel knew the story. 'Roca, pretty boy, looks after the affairs of the Hapsburgs. He worked for them in Paris.'

He added Gyp had at one time worked on the frontier. Of course, he was a cop.

I asked Gyp later if this was the case and realizing I knew something of his past he agreed working with the military police had brought him into contact with many aspects of the key, the journey. With his men he had patrolled the wild terrain from the

Pyrenees Mountains to the Mediterranean Sea and had crossed over on many nights into France.

'The whole thing is not Girona.'

And that was not his whole story either, I thought.

The phone call came for me at 5 p.m. as I sat on a cool bench outside the hotel and I expected it to be the custodian. José said he was concerned with what he had been hearing. I asked immediately where he was.

'Out of Girona. You must stay away from this idea. You cannot be part of the society. Certainly not a custodian.'

I asked why not.

'You don't speak Catalan.'

I said I could learn.

'Do not do this.' It appeared Dr Arnau had asked him to call. I told him Gyp was trying to displace him.

'He can try,' he said. 'Stay out of this.'

'Why?'

'Otherwise you will never get out of this.' He said he thought of me and hung up.

22

Ten sharp, he was there in the hotel breakfast room, as sharp as the hour, crisp and ready for whatever the day brought him. He said we had to be there before midday. I asked where and why.

'Because of the light. À midi, pommes bleues.' He smiled, the one he used with Kathleen and the photographs and I remembered her words, 'Never underestimate that man.'

Why didn't I get rid of Gyp? Could I? I didn't know yet who he was and he had the statue of the slant-eyed figure holding the crescent moon. I phoned the custodian and left a message saying I needed help. I could see there was no virtue in blocking the expedition.

I took a seat next to Gyp and asked him what happened to Peter Jack. He frowned and looked surprised.

'You remember that guy on the deluge afternoon in the cafe Antigua who was going to make a film? It seemed he got discouraged.'

'You can write a better one.'

'Did you buy him off? The society got into it?'

'You don't need him. The next book you will write will be this story, the untold story of Girona.'

In the mirror he saw my face. I guess I didn't look like someone who was going to write any books.

Surprisingly we didn't go to Mount O but the other side with Joseph's grave, not far to the left.

He pointed to Mount O directly behind the convent and then handed round several pairs of binoculars. I assumed we would go up the track afterwards. Gyp looked at his watch and said the light would change at any time, heightening to maximum in 15 minutes. He checked everyone's use of the binoculars and adjusted mine and said to keep focused on the hut halfway up the slope. I was somewhere between disliking him or myself for even being here. I wanted to get back at him but I was far from sure I would win. In English I said, 'You won't win. José always reignites his life.' I couldn't see his expression because his binoculars covered his eyes. The light struck the point on Mount O ten minutes before midday and yes, there was a trace of blue in a semi-circle between those trees. Just a hint. Was it because I expected to see it?

'I can see it,' said Cathy thrilled.

'Why aren't we over there?' said the actor.

Gyp explained that the view was correct from this angle. We wouldn't see the Stones become visible from over there. Yes, they were stones. 'Sixteen. The descendants of the family that has been guarded for 2000 years.' Cathy and Piers could make out several Stones with traces of blue.

'If it's the claim that Henry Lincoln made in the *Holy Blood and the Holy Grail*, forget it,' said the actor. 'And that bloodline film has been condemned as fake. Even the writer admits it. He faked the lot. An investigator, Lewis Doyle, broke that story. And if there is a bloodline of Jesus and the Magdalene what of it? It would be so diluted now, thousands upon thousands of people would be descendants.'

He was too busy talking and missed the Stones altogether.

Piers did, it seemed, believe in the claim. Gyp kept his silence. Cynthia said, 'This is bigger than you and José. There are highly established people behind Gyp.' The blue light faded and Piers and the actor were ready to go to Mount O.

'Not possible,' said Gyp. 'Private property. You are the first to see this blue emerge and know what it is. Look! It is quite gone now.'

The problem was one woman had seen it and Anna only thought she might.

The actor was going to be trouble and I reminded him, Blue Apples were not on the itinerary. And it occurred to me finally what Gyp was doing. With one hand I was the next custodian but he would pay no public lip service to my work or José. He was rewriting the script. I told the group I used the legends and the local street stories to find the truth. The key places were the convent, the grave, the Barraca where Hughes and Rahn had visited, and Charlemagne had stayed. Gyp was watching me and I could see my number was up.

'It's about duplication,' he said. 'You confuse the issue. I am trying to show you the way.'

'Have you duplicated the translator? I don't see Roca today.'

Piers took his attention and they walked towards the cars.

Quickly I asked the photographer who had been there the first day, about the oriental figure on the patio of the meeting house. Where had the owners acquired that? My accent or the subject confused him and I had to get Cathy and tell her to keep it subdued. Gyp, perhaps sensing intrigue, was freeing himself from Piers's questions. 'Ah, yes. The female carrying the scroll,' agreed the photographer.

'With slanting eyes?'

'Shadowed,' he said. 'You can't see the eyes.'

I quickly said, 'Could we go now and look at the statue and not say anything to Gyp?' He hadn't had a request like this. What did I want?

Gyp, now in a stern mood came back, asked the photographer to take a car and drop us at the hotel as he now had things to do. Would we see him again? He didn't say.

The car filled up and I quickly asked the photographer if it was Gyp's house. He said it was privately owned. I asked where the statue had come from and he didn't know, only that it was old. We started driving back to the city.

'It's not Catalan?' I said.

'Not at all, no.'

'But you said the female carries a baby,' said Cynthia.

He remembered a scroll.

'And a garment made of flowers? Eyes slanted?'

Then he got a good idea. Why didn't we ask Gyp? He was never going to go into that house.

'How come Gyp gets in?'

He thought about that. 'Because he's the guardian.'

119

We went into the hotel and Cathy asked to speak to me privately. 'I spoke to Gyp and asked who he works for. He was reluctant to talk about it but it seemed not anybody in this town. He told Piers he gets orders.'

'So, it's Central Intelligence?'

'Let's hope that's what it is. I would play it carefully. Just a feeling,' she said.

The Calvary was on a pleasing stretch of land to the side of Mount O, twelve tombs around the small closed church of Saint Stephen.

'Everything is duplicated,' Gyp told the group. He pointed to the last and largest cross.

'Pousin's tomb and here in Rennes'—he skillfully unfolded Boudet's map—'the tomb of Poussin. Over there, Mount O. In Rennes'—he turned the map around—'Mount Cardou.'

These landmarks could be identical. The woman from Arkansas said, 'Are we being had or are we being had?' The group was now divided.

'But Poussin is buried in Rome,' said the actor.

'He could be buried anywhere,' said Gyp. 'But his tomb is here and another in Rennes.' Using pure power he silenced the actor and allowed no further interruption.

The USA woman walked noticeably towards the actor. 'I know what he does. He's an interrogator,' she said.

I thought she had something there. Why was I still here? There was no place for me to speak this afternoon.

Cynthia nudged me. 'Why don't you just ask him about the deal? When do you get the property?'

Gyp paused. Had he caught that? I was beginning to think like Roca. Bugs. Sensors.

What was the point of duplication? To double the strength of the passage between the two identical points? Was it like the reverse hotel rooms? Was the purpose to get used to a double way of looking in preparation for the journey? Were two points all there was? Did they join also in an upward line becoming a triangle? A pyramid?

Gyp was talking of the St Daniel convent as though it was his.

I remembered going with José years ago and walking in the cloisters and how these women liked him and he wrote of them in his poems. He saw the beauty in their life. As a child he'd gone often to eat with them when his grandmother was not there. José had introduced this place to Gyp, of that I was sure. It was part of the legend of the city, nicknamed the Bank or Caja of Girona. It dealt with money. And why?

About that there was a mystery. And the tomb of Joseph of Arimathea. They said he was buried somewhere in the valley. He was a tin merchant and had come here after the Crucifixion. There was metal of all kinds in this province so it would be a place he might visit. I now understood there was a great deal of travel in those days. And José had said the grave was his but he may not be in it. He could have allowed another he loved to be buried there. Or employ it for initiations. The initiate would lie the night in that grave and the teacher would appear at daylight and if the initiate's account of what he had seen, feared, thought, dreamed, matched the desired requirement he had passed that part of the test.

Gyp, now beside me, no doubt wondering why I was so quiet. I had been so in love with José in those days I'd not paid much attention to the setting. Gyp looked at the crosses and through them the beloved city in the distance. 'José used to come here. He loved this place.'

And by his tone I knew he had once loved José, maybe had been his student. What had gone wrong?

23

I took off, alone, up the Calle Forsa to the house where I'd been taken at the beginning of the week when I was the person I used to be. Now I was in it, someone else's illusory goal, the only way out was through it. I knew that. I tried to get into the property by ringing bells, banging on the two doors. I tried to see the patio from the street. You saw nothing of that property, however you looked. I carried on walking without aim and realized instinctively I was going to the Barraca. It would be the logical place of recovery. Yet I kept on down the track to the fountain and the St Daniel district.

Exhausted I sat by the fountain and remembered it as it used to be, a simple place to get water. A man came towards me with a cup. He paused and asked if I was thirsty. He had a distinguished face, exceptional eyes, with an intensity of expression that was rare. His hair was long to his collar and swept back at the sides. He wore traditional espadrilles and simple, clean clothes. He seemed gentle and sat beside me on the step. I tried to think of what to say. There was nothing to say. He was the custodian from Ripoll, Dr Arnau, of that I was sure.

'Shall I get you more water?' he asked

I thanked him and held up the cup. He pointed to the steps opposite. 'It's called Jacob's ladder and that house belonged to José Tarres' mother. It was a "merinda". Do you know what that is?'

I did not.

'A place where you go and drink tea in the afternoon. And in the evening they had dances by the river.'

I thought the description stirred a memory but too buried to retrieve.

He looked younger than he'd sounded on the phone. There was so much I would have needed to tell him but in his company it all seemed irrelevant. I supposed I'd reached a deeper, more restful state. How long we stayed in silence I could not have said. I recalled the Folch sisters saying he was charismatic and his students fell for him.

I felt calm and safe and it was suddenly a good afternoon.

I had decided to look for a church to ask a priest for an answer and here I sat in a once-loved place and one came to me. I said, ' "This is the last day of the rest of my life." I heard somebody say this the other day. I thought, that's me.'

'Perhaps you are on the way to start again.'

'If only that was possible. I thought it meant I was going to die.'

'Most people dread that thought.'

'What do you do?' I decided to ask.

'Part of it is to help people to die.' He said it so simply I wanted to cling to him, beg him to keep me safe. I took hold of his hand.

'You do know Gyp Planas, don't you?'

'Your guide, Liliane, gave a timely warning about Portals. The experience gives a richness of insight, a certain freedom but should never be approached alone. Always go to the Portal with a guide after considered preparation otherwise this privileged experience can be unwise. Gyp Planas should be careful.'

Portal? Had it all to do with a Portal?

'Do you believe what he says?'

'Some of it.'

'Why?'

He laughed. 'Because he got it from me, and I from my teachers. José also helped him.'

'Are the Stones, Blue Apples, descendants of Jesus and the Magdalene?'

A laugh answered that.

He touched my arm as he left. 'I will be in touch.'

As I went through the revolving doors of the hotel, Gyp was waiting on the black slippery couch.

'You must understand,' he said immediately, 'that to be in the role prepared for you, work has to be done. You have to learn to be obedient.'

'Who owns the house where you held that meeting?'

'For me these questions are no problem but they eat time. Time we do not have.' He got up. 'Let's go.'

I did not move.

'So, who looks after you, Gyp? You mention this property is mine: the house, the gardens. Who provides that?'

'The society. They will do everything for you.'

'José when he comes back to Girona might have a different view.'

'Not even important. He will not even have a house. The society will not go on paying him to change his mind more than most do their underpants. Now let's go.'

I still did not get up.

'I have done a great deal for José. More than you can think,' he added as he left.

Yes, he had been let down.

I hadn't asked Gyp about his private life because he never left space. His private life was his own. I felt that boundary was set and I would know absolutely nothing about him. I felt those number fives, for his invisibility that Masia collected for him, must work. Was he married? Children? Happy? Was he wealthy? Well off ? On his uppers? Did he still work? Did he go with women? I thought he spent his energy on showing what he'd collected to get me to be the acquiescent custodian he could use. For what purpose I did not know. Yet.

Gyp came into the restaurant and I knew it was him because of the way other diners looked up from their food. He was either claiming all attention or invisible. He sat down with us but refused to eat or drink.

'I hear you have again shown an interest in the statue on the patio of the Casa Cundaro.' He sounded disappointed.

So the photographer had talked. 'I saw one thing. You tell me it's another.'

'So, come with me. Let's go and look.' He got up and the others left with us, their desserts forsaken. For a moment he wasn't sure about them but got into the car leaving space for three slim ones in

124

the back seat. Somewhere before the Casa Cundaro he seemed to change his mind and backed off, taking a longer route. It wasn't yet dark and he drove through St Daniel before turning back towards the town. Why the diversion? A lock and chain across the track stopped any progress. He leapt out, took a bunch of keys from a pocket, tried two, was successful on the third and the chain dropped to the ground. He got back in the car, drove onto the track, got out and relocked the chain. I was glad I wasn't alone with him. Piers was impressed. A lock and key for all occasions.

Matter of fact, he said, 'I can go anywhere in this city. No door keeps me out.' The track led to the Mount O and he parked the car behind the Moroccan restaurant. Quickly, without speaking, he took my hand and we all climbed up an overgrown track until it was impossible to go further.

'Behind us, the Blue Apples,' he said. 'But you can't go through this undergrowth. Now you have the proof. I will cut it for you. Would José do that?' He looked out across at Girona, his face not without pain. Yes, he loved this city, which in turn must have hurt him. We got back down and into the car.

'But it will be too dark to see the statue,' I said. Wasn't that what he wanted? More delaying tactics while he made a phone call. Then we arrived at the fountain with the Lady with the Pear.

Keys opened several locks and we were inside the original room with the spinning photographs. Upstairs to the patio and there we abruptly stopped in front of the statue. She didn't hold a scroll as the photographer thought and she didn't have slanted eyes either. No crescent moon cradled in arms, thin as sticks. This woman held a child and was bigger, fleshy with breasts and a stomach. No halo. Nothing Christian about her. But she wasn't from the East either. It wasn't the same statue. I understood the diversion was to give time to switch it. Although it was almost dark I saw the scuff marks where a large stone object had been dragged across the patio and Gyp saw me seeing them. I should look elsewhere, avoid giving myself away but could not. I could just make out a scratch mark across the tiles but it was too dark to see more.

Where I looked he looked and our eyes eventually met. I had

125

just raised my game as they say. I understood why we had to spend so much time getting here. We could only visit this patio in darkness.

'Where is it from?' asked Piers.

'Istanbul,' said Gyp automatically.

'Not what I saw,' I said and walked out.

At the hotel he didn't leave the car and said he would be there tomorrow to say goodbye to Cathy and Piers. 'I cannot stay long. I have a lot to do. Dan Brown is coming Monday.'

'Dan Brown is coming Monday.' Piers echoed the sound of these dismal words like some deadly mantra.

Although it was late, I phoned Dr Arnau and said Gyp was too much for me. Was it true Dan Brown was being offered the material? Please could he find out? I'd now reached a new level of distress I didn't know existed. Dr Arnau said to stay calm and he would deal with it. Short and sharp. I wasn't sure what he meant.

A night of swirling half dreams, statues that switched from Ethiopian to Chinese to Christian spinning round as the photographs from the first day. I plunged into a heap of stick arms and crescent moons.

Dan Brown didn't have the story. Dan Brown could buy the story.

24

Piers drew lines between the five places we had been shown and explained how Gyp had found each point by measurements of 110, 210 and in some cases 310 metres. Lines of control ran crossways, lengthways and this was as it should be. No thick pencil here. Where was the constellation of the Great Bear? He suggested I ask José. I was one ahead and would ask the custodian. I would do it privately and keep the information to myself. In normal times I would not distrust Piers but trust was no longer an option I could engage with. I had to claim the role of custodian if it was mine. I remembered Gyp's words that I would never be free.

Piers's knowledge was calmly explained and well researched. He spent his life working on metaphysical subjects with an expertise not often found in these circles. His teachers were considered exemplary and he had an academic background and what he'd done between university and this present year, when he became involved in Rennes, I did not know. Characters in the metaphysical world seemed to have fallow areas, which had no necessary explanation.

'The Blue Apples is the most exciting discovery in years,' he said. 'This is the answer to the insoluble mystery. What are the Blue Apples?'

I waited.

'Graves,' he said.

'Whose graves?'

'The descendants of Jesus and Magdalene.'

I didn't go along with that one, never had, since hearing of Henry Lincoln's claim in *The Holy Blood and the Holy Grail*.

'I would keep it quiet or everyone will be here swarming over Girona. They've been looking for this for the last 40 years,' he concluded.

Gyp didn't come at ten. He wasn't there at noon. Anna and I sat outside El Balco which served the best meat in town waiting for Piers's car and driver to take him to Rennes. He was sure what we'd been shown was the real thing and would be a sensation. Everyone would be after it. 'Start writing,' he said.

'Is that what Gyp wants? A book?' I asked.

'I don't know,' said Piers, 'but you do. You need a book before Dan Brown decides he does. You've worked for it. It's your story .'

'Do you believe Dan Brown is coming Monday?'

'Could be,' said Piers. 'Gyp needs to secure the material.'

'It's not his. It's José's,' I said.

I asked him who was behind Gyp. 'Didn't he say he gets orders?'

Piers did hesitate. 'But in the dark. Before he goes asleep, a beam of light comes through.'

Anna said at some point Gyp told her he wasn't afraid of death and that all the best ones were on the other side. He'd meant members of the society.

Cynthia didn't like the instructions from a beam-of-light-in-darkness story. 'He's working with the powers of darkness. Be careful.'

After lunch I called Masia and said I was on the way to the bookshop and needed to speak to him. He said he preferred to meet me somewhere discreet and chose a bar near the hotel. He arrived promptly and brought me a magazine about the St Daniel Valley in the last century. I asked how well he knew Gyp and he, as I suspected, sidestepped that question. So I jumped right to it and asked about the Blue Apples. I said I had always been told Mount O was a particular and special place. He said he had no proof but there was a group who met near the border and they were special. They were initiates and were said to have special blood.

'That of Jesus and the Magdalene?'

'That's what some people think.' What else could you think?

I asked if Gyp was part of this and he thought not. 'They meet every few months and have a ceremony to do with the past.'

'Witchcraft?'

'Oh, no. These are very highly evolved people.' He thought they came from near Figueres. 'They are a powerful group that want the world to be a better place. Apparently they can affect that.'

'How can I meet these people?'

He had no idea. He knew only the hearsay over the years. He remembered as a child being told they wore hoods and ritual dress. And they celebrated the new moon or they chose that time for their meetings. 'So I think it must be connected with the possible descendants.'

'Unless they are Cathars,' I said.

He was trying to be helpful and could not but see his invitation to meet Gyp had done me no good. I'd aged ten years. I asked how José would feel about my accepting Gyp's offer, the custodial role.

'They were quite close. I don't know about now.' He did. He had heard Gyp say José was finished. 'Gyp had been José's student. Gyp would do anything for him.'

'How did they know each other?'

He didn't know.

So I asked if Gyp was Central Intelligence. He said he wouldn't know that. I reminded him that he had a responsibility to me. His phone call got me into this.

'I only know he worked on the frontier and spent a lot of time in that area. Maybe that is how he got some of this material. And his men still work for him now. He keeps everything segregated. So I wouldn't know.'

So, how did Masia see me? Was their offer of custodian authentic? And was the society going to finance me staying in Girona?

'It must be, because suddenly that is what Gyp wants you to do. He is very set on that.'

I asked if Gyp had a wife and family.

'He's never mentioned that.'

'Oh, come on, Ramon. Even for a Catalan's sense of privacy that's going too far. You must at least have an opinion.'

'He's not a lot around Girona. I knew he had a mother in

Girona. There was talk, a long time ago, that he had had a young wife.'

I wondered if Ramon said as little about me.

I phoned Dr Arnau in the evening and said I hadn't seen Gyp Planas.

'That's what you wanted.' He sounded amused.

'Is it by chance?'

'No. I have spoken to some people.'

I said I understood Gyp was not close to José anymore and wanted me to follow the journey. I thought that covered everything.

'What journey?'

'The key.'

Dr Arnau said he did not know of any such key.

'It opens the lock of the secret. Is it the same key José mentioned many years ago?'

He paused and chose to give me some information.

'The key is not a key in that way. It is a *vesica piscis*.'

I asked what that was.

'Two overlapping circles. I doubt if Gyp knows of that.'

He wouldn't know from me.

25

Gyp was nowhere in sight. Was he out in the valley showing Dan Brown other more exotic graves, or digging mine? I was sure that intercession from Ripoll had not pleased him. Why had he brought Dan Brown into this?

'He's stirring you up,' Anna assured me and I thought it was time for her to go back to her clients in London.

Roca called the hotel and asked me to meet him in a nearby bar. He looked less glossy than previously, and it turned out his eyes were not blue but hazel light-brown with green flecks. The contact lenses had been for the job. He had been advised by the Dali administration to carry on his life and not be nervous of Gyp.

'The more energy I give him with my fear, the worst he becomes. If I just drop him from my thoughts, he will vanish.' He snapped his fingers. At that precise moment a Land Rover thundered past the open door, filled with men with ropes and shovels, some hanging onto the sides. It had all the appearance of a Gyp Planas' operation. I turned to Roca but he was gone. He was crouched behind the table. 'Just habit,' he said and got back to his seat. Anna said it was a dust cart and got his attention on Dan Brown and the people who would know if he was coming on Monday. He went into the street and spent more than five minutes calling on his mobile. He came back and said neither the mayor's office or the local press knew about it. He clicked his phone shut and recovered his good form. I didn't believe I'd got the full Gyp-offering-a-job story but there was a quality in Roca: a purity, an integrity, which I felt made it impossible to blur the truth.

'Dan Brown hasn't got the story,' I said. 'He doesn't know the people.'

'Maybe not,' said Roca. 'But he can buy the people.'

When I asked again in what way Roca had been approached he

said he'd been told about a man with metaphysical interests like his and he was from an old Templar family. 'But when I asked Masia, he didn't know him.'

'That figures. He never knows anything until you know it.'

'How come you'd never heard of Gyp? You come from Girona,' said Anna.

'I've been away from here several years. Don't forget,' he said sharply, 'I just came back.'

'From where?' said Anna.

'Many places. Shall I send you my CV?'

I could see the beginning of unnecessary trouble and asked him what happened next.

'Gyp came into the bookshop. I was sitting in the back talking to Masia's daughter. He was just suddenly there. Like he hadn't done the normal thing of coming in.'

I knew (how I did) what he was describing.

'He had a kind of attitude. "I'm here so be ready. Life will never be the same for you." Masia introduced us and he did a bit of PR, because Gyp liked my Dali connection and the fact I'd travelled and was good in English. He talked about you and said you were OK, but getting old and needed our help. He said to contact you and fix a meeting. I thought I'd forward on a photocopy I'd just received from a Hapsburg friend from Budapest. "Look at this, well", I thought it would intrigue you.'

He wasn't wrong.

'I was to look after you at Gyp's matinee performance.'

'Did he mention José?'

'Gyp said José was too old.'

There's a lot of old in the story. Has he looked in the mirror lately?

'I wanted to meet you first and tell you something about it. He used sensors and worked in CI, maybe, still does. One of the men said he used to scour the frontier obsessively, night after night. I am relieved to be out of it. He has something that scared me. I thought of going to the police but he is the police.'

I asked what he was looking for on the frontier.

'Something he'd heard was there. Spanish side, French side, he was hopping both ways. Surveillance is his thing.'

I showed him the photocopies of the grave of Joseph of Arimathea, and that's when he started laughing. He had a wonderful, effortless laugh.

'The grave is also in Glastonbury. How can it be in two places?' I said.

'Everything else is,' said Roca. 'Let's hope we're not.'

He examined the picture of the grave under the light. 'He's got the idea from a juvenile history thriller. He's probably put a bottle with a scroll between the rocks. At least you haven't got to find that. Dan Brown gets to do it. The scroll in the rocks. They pull that every season in Rennes.'

'The grave was too small. Not even a corpse could get in,' said Anna. 'It's an animal trap.'

Roca agreed although he'd never seen it. 'The sort of thing I could see him doing.'

'I've seen the same in France. It's a trap for sangliers,' she said.

Roca was impressed. 'Do you know what you are saying? Sanglier — Sangral. How appropriate is that? It all fits. Gyp at his best.'

'A sanglier is a wild boar,' explained Anna, in case there was any confusion.

'So, that's all he's got, a sanglier in a stone trap passing it off as Joseph of Arimathea. That's going to please Dan Brown. Gyp couldn't find the bones of the biblical figure, so catches, by mistake, a wild boar. That fits. Dan Brown's going to love that.'

Gyp's absence worried me more than his presence. I phoned José's number and he answered.

'I am not safe.'

He didn't argue with that. 'Go to the place of the skull.'

'Skull? The altarpiece? Joseph of Arimathea's grave?' I wasn't thinking straight.

'Further north. The place where I held the skull on the hill.'

I noticed he hadn't said the place name. Was he concerned, too, about being bugged? The sensors? Mustn't forget those.

And then I remembered Rebés, the old village near the frontier. And outside the village a sloping hill and an abandoned hamlet. There was a chapel, a graveyard, a phone box, a small school, an old house, a board with local notices blowing in the wind, and there was a Stone Cradle.

Years ago, José had gone there on a mission and taken me with him. As we arrived it was as though the place had just been vacated. The door of the school was still swinging and we watched it close. José had knelt in the overgrown grass and a skull rolled towards him. 'Look at this,' he said with curiosity and he picked it up as though to see whom it had been. I told him to put it down, to wash his hands immediately. And he took no notice and turned the skull round in his hands in a friendly way, wishing it well and placed it near a grave.

He brushed his hands on his trousers then saw my expression and took a clump of weeds to clean them. 'These are herbs and antiseptic,' he said.

Who else had been in the car? Yes, the other was the man from Ripoll, Dr Arnau. And of course, there was the Stone Cradle. Was that why we were there? It was more than 20 years ago.

I couldn't go there now. They would follow me.

If Gyp wanted something from me he would be watching me. The something he needed? What was more obvious than the Stone Cradle? That was the end story, the piece he presumably didn't have. Roca had been told he'd sought something along the frontier hopping from one side to another. I must keep very quiet. I must be the person with little knowledge, intent now on returning to my usual life. Rebés was an hour away but Gyp knew the police, had worked with them, probably had the chief already in his pocket.

And then the phone rang and I expected it would be José.

Dr Arnau told me to go to a small place near Nîmes in France and take the small local train south from there, direction: Saintes-Maries-de-la-Mer, get out at Aigues-Mortes and I would be met by a priest. 'You will be made well there. We won't fail you. You are valued. Do not go to Rebés and I'm sure you won't speak to

134

anyone about José's suggestion or of ever being there.' He was obviously not concerned about sensors. 'Just think about your grandchildren and how much delight you get with them. I saw recently a photograph of the girl, your granddaughter. Is she only 12? She looks just like you.'

It wasn't until I got to Nîmes that I started to recover. In Aigues-Mortes on this rainy day, sitting in the huge bedroom with its walls of stone at the Templars Hotel filled with absolute silence, I was healed. The silence was old and had built up over many years. It had a noise like a whirring that filled my ears. The rain falling steadily so freeing, so refreshing. Being in that silence was like lying against thick cream. I felt held and absolutely as I should be. The priest found me the next day and I was glad to listen to him but the healing was done.

26

Lewis Doyle was on the phone before I'd got in the door. Had I accepted the role? What was the secret? The journey? Different to the one to the Portal? I asked him if he had heard of a Stone Cradle. He was struck silent.

'Let me think about it. Let me take a look at Gyp's photocopies.'

Seeing how he might react to the wild boar grave, I thought, better not.

Piers offered to help in any way he could. I asked him what a Stone Cradle meant. Nothing. We agreed a cradle was an object that held and comforted: the cradle of Moses made of bulrushes, the Christmas crib. Cradles were not hard. We agreed the word was more used as an adjective. 'To cradle an infant' or a noun, 'the cradle of civilization'. I did some research and there had been a stone cradle in Ephesus, Turkey which had been made off with, probably by the Knights Templar. It was quite small. I did recall the dark-blue smooth stone in Rebés. It was satisfying to the touch and shaped like a fruit dish. Large? Enough to lie in. I knew (how I did). I had to keep this information to myself. The Stone Cradle had been elegant and slim, and beautifully crafted. It rocked on a base of solid material of what, I could not recall. Was Dan Brown ensconced in Girona providing Gyp with all the money and power that he wanted? Was Dan Brown actually in Girona? Lew was the one to ask. He checked it out with 'his people' and they said Dan Brown had the Catalan flag on one of his websites.

I was asked to do a talk for the Rennes group in Soho and I saw the point of claiming the material now. Lew said focus on the Blue Apples' discovery. Put it on social media.

I established from Masia that they were rectangular stones. Had he seen them? It was impossible to get up there. For him. The Blue Stones were laid out in a semi-circle around Mount O.

'Why are they there?'

136

'Nobody knows. There is a gazebo there, a summerhouse. You can see it amongst the trees. Gaudi—' he waited for me to prove I knew who that was, yes, the extraordinary Catalan designer—'he used to come there.'

I asked Masia why and he believed it was for private meetings. 'You could sit there in the cool of the summer and talk and no one would overhear you.'

I wondered what Masia was going to get out of all this.

'Some people say Gaudi built the summerhouse,' he added.

I asked again what the site was used for. He still did not know. He would know when I knew.

He did sound a little chastened. No laughter today. Before he hung up I asked if the Blue Apples marked graves of the descendants of the Magdalene and Jesus. For example, those people who met near Figueres in robes and hoods at the time of the new moon.

'I wouldn't know that.'

Finally I asked about Gyp. He still hadn't seen him and he was supposedly busy with a writer from the US. Suddenly furious I said if he'd asked me to be the custodian why bring in Dan Brown? Masia said Gyp did what Gyp wanted. It took some days to reach Dr Arnau.

'Remember, you have been shown the way,' he said. 'Think back to the village, near the border in France.'

I remembered crystalline light and large circles, one after the other, appearing just above the land; silvery white, fairy circles, one overlapping the other and we watched, the man on the hill and the farmers. Couldn't remember much else.

'Like crop circles,' I said.

'No,' said Dr Arnau. 'But think crop circles and you will get there.'

When he'd hung up I looked again at the talisman of the oriental figure cradling the crescent moon. Was it the sculpture I had seen on the patio?

According to Roca, José was glowing as though reborn. They had met in the Arc bar. 'He understands me like no one else does.'

I cut through all that and asked what he said about Gyp.

'I told him Gyp is an enemy but he couldn't care less. He says Gyp is now in dark energy but the light will always win and Gyp will burn out. He will not talk about the Blues Apples. The subject is not up for discussion. The society won't do anything to stop Gyp because they will just let him do all this and then hang by his own rope. There is no sign of Gyp. Maybe he slipped down a Portal.'

So I asked if he'd remembered to check on the José-going-to-Paris-story and he said of course he remembered. He'd written down all my questions before the meeting. 'José was going to a society member in France, the visit organized by Dr Arnau. Gyp had worked for the society so would know this. He had been the guardian and had used his men from his police days, but he started taking over, became ambitious. José does not want you in this.'

'I am in this.' It now made sense why Gyp had rushed everything, had taken me with such speed into the Casa Cundaro that first day so no one should see or object. For all he knew, José may not have taken the train and could be right there, behind me.

'José needs you to be safe. He has always had this special love for you.'

Immediately he was off the phone, I called José and asked about Rebés. He said it was safe for me and always had been.

'So the Stone Cradle is the end story?'

'If you like. Or the beginning.'

I asked about the white circles.

'They are a part of the landscape. Celestial ley lines. One on the earth, the other slightly above. They are an indication of what is to come. The overlapping point is the Cradle. Remember it and remember Gyp does everything for Gyp. He has been looking for the Stone Cradle for years.'

'Why wasn't he shown it?'

'He wasn't ready and now he will never be ready.' I asked if he would come to Rebés with me.

'Not obviously, but in spirit I will.'

No leaving this table. Better win. I had the end story. Gyp did not. I must take control and speed up. Dr Arnau would not elaborate on the Stone Cradle. It was prehistoric and not a place of pilgrimage. A sacred place. But not for Gyp Planas. He paused. I didn't like his pauses. I thought in one of these I would meet my end. He would disconnect from me. He asked if I had meditated on the journey to Rebés and what had I seen? I dreaded those with commercial interests taking what was mine. I was referring to Dan Brown. He said I should return to the meditation he had suggested. Finally, I mentioned the talisman, the oriental figure cradling the crescent moon. No pause now. He asked how I'd found it. No finding anything here. It came from Budapest.

'I will be in touch with you.' No pause getting off that phone.

I started with the circles, the *vesica piscis* and let them loose on Piers. He got busy with the research, and believed, as many did, that the Magdalene had a child by Jesus. He, as Kathleen McGowan, Ani Williams, Andy Gough and many more as far as I knew, believed in the bloodline. I did not. Jesus was a divine being, on this Earth to teach us, to help us reach a new level of evolvement. He was not here to propagate children. If, as some believed, he had not been crucified and had fled to France would such a person hide in a cave? The world would know of his existence. He would be carrying out his ministry. My beliefs put me in a minority in this metaphysical group and they looked on me as a sucker for the falsehoods of the man-made church. I had a slight sense of how it was in the past to have un-receiveable ideas. Piers gave me books on the Magdalene and he was sure she was the Lady with the Cup that appeared periodically in Girona. Andy Gough from *Mindscape* wouldn't let me finish what I believed. 'Jesus was a Jewish rabbi and in that religion they were obliged to marry. Of course, he had a child.' For him and the rest, the Blue Apples were the descendants.

I knew José believed in Christ as I did. It wasn't a belief, it was to 'know.'

I revisited Rebés in my thoughts and believed, in one of the earlier visits, I had eaten in the small restaurant which seemed to be the only one in this enclosed village. I remembered the owner who served our group was surly even though the men were Catalan. Then we drove to the hill and the expensive car got a little roughed up on the unkempt track.

On the mound at the top there was an abandoned settlement: a chapel, a school, a public telephone, a listing of local notices, an old substantial house, some graves, a skull. Yes, the sound of Gregorian chants through the trees. The wind was strong. It was an open space with a view. Not sure about the view. And the door of the school was still moving and we watched it stop and close. And José held the skull and there was nobody there, yet there was a feeling of not being quite alone.

The long winding road to the distant hamlet. It is hard to traverse this ancient territory with is powerful winds, storms and uneven narrow tracks, where people are not welcome

The Stone Cradle was behind the house. Was it inside a small chapel or a plain, stone building like a sheep croft? It was a smooth, dark-blue stone like soft marzipan, a rocking cradle big enough to lie in. Carreras was there and other men. Carreras was a

140

priest just returned from South America and José said he was from the society. What did the men talk about? I only knew I loved José to the death. I had no idea this rocking stone had any importance and yes, I had seen it before on another visit. I tried to take his hand, to take him away from the group. I wanted to be alone with him, I wanted him. Maybe it was more than 20 years ago. For a while I could not bear to remember that passion and I think I did at that time ask God to take it into his care because I could not handle this. The cradle did rock and there were objects around it, a long oil-light and one of the men said it was pre-Christian, but not as old as the Cradle.

Now in London, whatever I was doing, my thoughts were always drawn back to the abandoned hamlet.

Yes, there had been a public fountain for drawing water. I phoned Dr Arnau and told him about the fountain and he said, 'Now you can begin.'

Begin?

'The journey.' Before I could ask where, he said, 'You will receive an invitation.'

I waited some days in anticipation. What I did get was an email showing a key and beside it a lock. And the message, 'Remember Cocteau.' Key and lock. After a while I considered the letter from Jean Cocteau to José saying he was the key and José the lock. Cocteau was referring to the metaphysical aspects of Girona. Who had sent the image? An email address in Budapest. I asked Dr Arnau if this was my invitation and he laughed and said it would arrive when I was ready. I would get clarification on the key and the lock if I considered that maybe Girona was the lock. So where and what was the key?

'The *versica pisces*,' he replied.

In the middle of the Rennes' presentation I received a text from Roca. 'Dan Brown probably in Girona.'

I was shaken to the point of silence and had to go outside. Anna said, 'It's Gyp. He's put out a rumour.'

'But there must be something to it. He's a Central Intelligence op.'

141

'He's a fantasist.' She was a mind-reader because she said, 'You're another one if you rush now to Girona.' I was already reaching for my debit card to buy the ticket.

I couldn't make sense myself of why I was so incredibly upset. I'd been betrayed. Obviously the society was fragile, dying off and no match for the Dan Brown empire. I would lose 'it'. The 'it' I didn't yet have. It obviously had appealed to me in spite of the manner of arrival in my life. It had been so unexpected. Another email—'Petite Bergère—little shepherdess, you alone hold the key. From the one who loves you best, Gyp.'

I phoned him immediately and he said to come to Girona. The secret was mine. Yes, Dan Brown had stayed at the Hotel Arts, Barcelona and they had discussed many things. 'But not the journey. That is yours. You are the custodian. I am cutting a path to the Blue Apples for you.'

27

Gyp waited on the Calle Forsa with Masia beside him as he had on that first day but they were now smiling. The absentee Roca was obviously not missed and his whereabouts not known. They were not a mystery to me. He waited in my room at the hotel. Gyp said something complimentary about my appearance, which I was supposed to hear as he said it in French. His eyes got a touch harder as he saw Anna come into sight beside me. He hadn't expected that. But then I'd been promised the mayor and he wasn't waiting on the street. The usual greetings, and into a restaurant on the Calle Forsa, and Gyp went straight to the kitchen, put his briefcase down proprietarily and lifted lids on pots cooking on the stove. We sat around a table for six giving us more space and Gyp immediately laid out a dozen photocopies. I was here, present and pleasant, because I was going to be shown the key, the whole 220 kilometres key. That was the deal. I said we should eat quickly and get going. We had probably seven hours of light left.

He took no notice of that and chose a photocopy. '5,521 years ago something happened here. It was the dawn of the great cycle. Pleiades on the meridian, the sun now preceded by a new star.' He stabbed a finger at the lines coming from the heavens to earth in triangles. 'The new morning star, Venus.' He turned the page so we all saw it equally. 'Venus, as it rose over the horizon. August, 3114 BC. In just under two months on 22 December 2012 it is the end of the great cycle and just before sunset the Pleiades will rise on the eastern horizon and Venus sinks below the western horizon.' His voice lowered caressingly. 'This is the symbolic death of Venus, indicating the start of a new processional age. Just further north, a matter of one hour by car, a Being of light was released from Venus and landed here in an area this side of the frontier with France, 5,521 years ago. This Being crashed through the atmosphere with a purpose.' He used the numeral Lew had generously given me. He took his pen away from the paper and looked straight into my eyes.

Oh, shit, I thought. He's found the Stone Cradle.

'To teach us. To raise our consciousness to its highest level. I am telling you this and to your secretary.'

I instinctively looked around. He meant Anna. I could see by her expression and its slow recovery that we had made a bad start to the new beginning. Several Beings crashing through the atmosphere could hardly be worse than the demoting of my critic and superior to the role of secretary.

'I am giving you this information because you have written about it and you are familiar with rebirth. You've published the book *Mr Lazarus*.'

He obviously had not read it. It had been published some months before by Andrew Gough, Heretic Publishing.

'Who was this Being?' He wasn't asking us.

He picked up another photocopy. I expected a face. I thought I was looking at a tower or an ET? 'You know this because you lived steps away in the Calle St Clara at number seven in 1975.'

Did I? Was I next to this tower thing? Did the Being of light live there? I looked suitably perplexed and Masia thought it all right now to start eating the olives. Gyp placed the photocopy in front of me like a death sentence. 'The tower of St Lucia.'

A Gyp pause, and I wondered if we could open the menus. I was aware of time passing and the ration of light being eaten away.

'The tower is who?' He was asking me?

God, they all wanted to get me doing their thinking. 'The custodian, Gyp, Roca?'

'Lucifer!' He shuffled the papers away and opened the large, hard-covered menu.

So, I'd lived next door to Lucifer? I tried to catch my new secretary's eye. Her role would lead me quite soon into hysterical laughter but she was still picking herself up from this ego-blow I would no doubt suffer from at a later time.

I chose fresh asparagus, fish and baked apple. I tried to remember 1975, the hideous year before José married. I said I'd drink water and Anna was not my secretary, but friend and a very experienced and sought-after psychoanalytical psychotherapist with a notable client list. He took no notice and said his star was Thuban. It had reigned as the previous pole star and another page was handed round. Thuban had shone directly onto Mount O, the site of the Blue Apples. I jumped on that and said I was looking forward greatly to the visit he'd promised me. I told Masia this was a pleasing reunion but we should get a move on. The fading light.

Gyp prodded the paper, demanding attention.

'So, Venus produced this Being which was fostered here. Why?'

I had no idea. My book *Mr Lazarus* didn't seem to cover this thing.

'Your friend, the custodian, seems to know everything and you run to him with bad stories about Gyp.' Talking about himself in the third person? Wasn't that a bad sign? Anna would know. Not now she wouldn't. Everyone at this table now condemned to third person with that unfortunate secretarial remark.

'You think the sophisticate Dr Arnau is going to give you the secret? You think Gyp doesn't know? That he's all lost in the dark? Not when I hold the knowledge of the Being of light. I bow to him and he gives me what I need. In front of him I can be a child.' Was this the beam of light in darkness? Wasn't Lucifer the devil? Was I off track? Masia nodded sagely. I thought it was the right time to start on the asparagus.

'You chose your friends yourself, shepherdess? Dr Arnau? You want to be careful. Maybe you should run them past your secretary.'

An icy silence as we buttered our bread.

'During the reign of Thuban—' the name began to sound like Anna and terrible laughter would be next—'the ground was prepared for the second arrival in this area. And that is what the world has been looking for down the ages and why the society shielded this knowledge.'

'The descendants?' I asked and wished my manner was more secure.

Gyp's voice continued, rich, sonorous, emotive, dark, always relentless. He heard questions but he did not reply. I told Masia the food was good. It was not, but he ate it as though it was. Gyp allowed a pause as he switched to his main plate that the owner had lovingly put in front of him and I jumped in with the essential matter. 'The key, Gyp. We have a problem.'

'No problem. You bring the problem.'

'Exactly,' hissed Anna. She wasn't nicknamed the Rottweiler for nothing.

'The key, Gyp. We have a problem,' she mimicked. 'You sound like his wife.'

Gyp allowed himself a moment of amusement. I nudged her and said speedily, 'The key is a *vesica piscis* — two circles.'

She ignored me, drank her coffee and started speaking. 'So the constellation is linked closely with this area?'

'Exactly,' said Gyp, and to me. 'Your secretary knows better than you.'

I stood up. 'Let's get on the road, understand the secret. I have only this day.'

Into the car and he started driving to the cathedral and round by the satanic windows. 'We cannot do it all in one afternoon,' he said. 'Tomorrow.'

'Now.'

Masia spoke to him and the car made a fresh U-turn. 'We'll make a start,' said Gyp. 'But you must understand, it's little by little. You have to be prepared for this. No impatience.'

I said we'd agreed on the phone I got it in one sweep. Masia tried to say there would not be sufficient time and then it occurred to me they were Catalan and very money conscious and I said I would pay for the petrol. Gyp said that was not necessary and we would go and see the Star of David unless I wanted the Tablets of Moses. Anna chose the first and we drove along the St Lazarus area and reached the church of St Pilar and got out.

146

He lowered his voice to do justice to the words. 'The key is very old. Saunière came here to claim it for the Hapsburgs.'

He started pulling me up a steep and muddied hill. I wondered how many slopes and hillsides I'd have to get up, to stay in the company of Gyp Planas.

After skirting around an industrial site manufacturing cement we turned up a perilous path full of holes, weeds, nettles, bracken and goat shit. Ahead of us a buxom woman in a long, rough skirt drove her line of goats forward with a stick. She smiled, showing one tooth and Gyp greeted her. He said he was going onto the next field. She understood him to say the next world and protested that he was too young. I could have had quite a disagreement with her. He came to his flock and she carried on with hers and he lead us clomping along a field, soon cut off by barbed wire. Shoes thick with mud, cement dust and dung, we reached a stretch of field protected by electric wire with signs showing a man electrocuted, dying and the word as if it was needed, 'Danger.' Of course, I had to touch the wire and found out the illustration was no exaggeration. Ten more minutes of impossible negotiation with the undergrowth and we still faced a muddied field enclosed by this electric wire.

'What exactly is this?' I asked.

'The Star of David.' And he stretched his arm to the horizon. 'It is laid out like a star.'

'You can see it from the plane,' said Anna, 'as you come into land. It's an odd shape. No one knows why it's there. It is huge.'

'I know why,' said Gyp. 'It's been laid there not by human hand so it's visible from above.' Masia's back was now out and he held onto the nearest thing, unhappily the wire. Gyp took no notice. 'We are walking on something that is magical.'

'Yes, in my case, shit.' I had no sense of being on the edge of any star.

I did remember it was suddenly visible 30 years ago and no one knew why. I had lost this day. I was now stuck on the edge of a field not remotely meant for human beings, I had been electrocuted, tripped up by tough weeds, stung by insects, embraced by

147

nettles, shoes heavy with muck, tired out. I would settle for the Blue Apples. Could it be worse? I turned round to go back and caused Masia to slip and we clung together as though in the middle of a desperate dance, rocking to and fro on a tiny island of dry earth. I did not know where next to put my feet. If this was where going on the secret journey led me, I was better off waiting for Dr Arnau and the invitation that still had not come. Anna and Gyp had to rescue us and once again I had Gyp's hands holding me up from danger. A little careworn we arrived at the car. Four of the seven hours' daylight gone.

'Blue Apples,' I said and we drove to Mount O.

This piece of history, overgrown and forgotten, was impossible to climb except for Anna who scaled mountains, sailed boats through impossible conditions, skied on Olympic slopes, dived from the high rocks into small pools. She ate reindeer. She was Norwegian, a Viking to the bone and Gyp saw all this and liked it. I reminded him he'd said he'd started clearing the path.

'But the municipality have to give a safe route for you. You are not able to go to that height unaided.' He looked at me regretfully. So it was my fault.

'Wednesday,' said Masia. 'The path will be cut Wednesday.' And then I got a good idea.

'Anna climbs. She could go up.'

Gyp shook his head. 'Not wise.'

'So you believe special descendants are here?'

I had hoped to surprise him.

He took my hand sorrowfully. 'It is not what I believe. It is what is.'

'So, how does that pan out in the real world?' I asked the 'secretary'.

'Just listen to him. He's trying to teach you something. He's doing his best,' she said. Oh, dear, she had decided to sleep with the enemy. I tried another question but he was off onto another subject. I said I hadn't come all this way and paid, to be here at the side of the road. I spoke to Masia and at least he listened. 'I want to go to Lucifer's place.'

Gyp caught that one and stopped mid-sentence.

'I'd settle to see the Being of light,' I said innocently. 'Where did it land? Where is it now?' And I walked to the car and got in.

The others followed and Gyp started the engine. He turned to Masia and suggested several places of interest.

'Just let's go north and see Lucifer,' I said sweetly.

Gyp's eyes slid sideways and looked at me. I could see them in the mirror, *Oh, so naive now, little shepherdess. Nice try.*

28

Later that evening I got them back on the road near the convent facing the Blue Apples. The photographer arrived with Gyp's assistant, Pepe, a man who cleared undergrowth and worked in the forest.

I was looking up the extent of Mount O and could see a crumbling building at the top, the church dedicated to the moon.

Anna said she would go up and she and Gyp, without ropes and torches, climbed as the mist rose.

'What a woman!' said Masia.

Pepe was looking up through the mist.

'Are you going up?' I asked him.

'Today it's not good. Bad for climbing.'

We could hear the crunch of branches, the rattle of stones as they climbed. Then nothing. 'We're there,' said Anna. 'You couldn't have got up here.'

'What's it like?' This I so wanted to know. 'Is it a graveyard?' She did not answer. Could I get up there? I looked at the beginning of the paths. On all fours? I started to try it and Pepe pulled me back.

'Not possible.'

'Don't come up, whatever you do!' Anna shouted. She didn't sound that far away. 'I will take photos. It's light up here.'

I wanted to put some questions to Pepe and started simply. 'Have you known about this place before?'

'It's always been known. José Tarres came here with my father. They played here as children.'

Gyp shouted he was coming down and Pepe shut up.

Mount O was terraced, exact and clear even through the undergrowth. 'Like an ancient temple,' said Pepe. 'The terrace goes all around the Mount, in circles.'

I said I thought it was for olives and grapes.

150

'No, no it is not agricultural.'

'So why is it terraced like this?'

'Because it would have been a place of –'

Masia cut across the answer. 'Let Gyp tell the story.'

Gyp and Anna were in sight as they swooped down, then up, disappeared in the hollows, stones sliding, branches cracking, Gyp holding her now, breaking the speed. And they were down, she carrying a Blue Stone, her cheeks flushed, eyes glowing.

'I couldn't have done it, not coming down without his help,' she said. She handed me the Stone, a fairly large rectangular tile, painted a cobalt-blue on the top. 'There are more than 16,' she said. 'Gyp found another four.'

That's a shame, I thought. Going to mess up the metaphysical lot and their 16 Blue Apples' prediction. Sixteen descendants?

I said, 'So they are the descendants of Mary and –'

'Jesus,' he said.

We stood quite still as though in respect, all Sunday-school teachings of my past shivering in awe of this terrible fraud. Which was guilty? This Mount? Or the church? 'So, there are graves up there?' I whispered. He nodded.

'We ought to get excavators in.'

He was quite surprised. 'To do what?'

'Verify the material.'

'Oh, I have people for that.'

Pepe took the Stone and looked at it one side, then the other, slowly. It seemed it was the first time he had seen one and he was amused she had brought it down. It was covered in white cement, with blue paint on top, inside a red tile. He said it could be any age but the paint was approximately 150 years. He said that they burned tiles like this in Roman times.

'So, you were the first to see the Blue Apples,' I told Anna, pleased for her. And she smiled, young, happy. 'What was it like up there?'

'Strange. Not what you'd think.' She gave me the Stone.

It was getting cold and the men wanted to leave. 'It is nearly November.'

'It's light-hearted up there,' she said. 'As though it was once a pleasure garden. I felt they'd play croquet up there. There's a summerhouse with old tiles and it's got a carefree atmosphere. The Stones were like shells in the ground, like a decoration. I've seen it before. It's as though they hold up the earth. That's how it looks.'

She showed a photograph and it had an atmosphere I had not known. It was a mixture of nostalgia, lightness and, yes, innocent. I needed to go up there but I sat on the ground holding the Stone and I felt this was a wondrous place, so unexpected, valuable, and by holding the Stone and being near to the Mount I was changed.

Gyp watched me and maybe saw the change. 'Better say a prayer.' And his hand moved towards mine and his eyes as they met mine were penetrating and deep and stirred me inappropriately. Just the tip of his fingers touched mine. An electric shock followed and it closed my eyes and shook my breathing. I pulled my hand away. 'I will pray for you,' he said softly. 'I always do.' And his voice—it sounded like a lover's. He had got the result he wanted and didn't need to do anything else. His voice changed as he straightened up and spoke to the men. And then he turned to the obedient secretary, 'Tomorrow, make sure she is ready. Tomorrow, punctual at ten o'clock you will be shown something exceptional. We go to the convent and you will be taken into the crypt. It holds documents and material hidden by the Knights Templar. No layperson has seen this,' he said my name. 'So, be punctual.'

29

Gyp and his men ate a quick dinner with us in the hotel. The earlier moment at Mount O had left no trace. He was back to the usual dominating controller who left little room for the opinions of others. Afterwards, I sat beside him on the fake leather sofa in the foyer. This was where I would sort it out.

'You say I am the custodian. Do you decide that?'

'No, you do, from birth.' Quick as a flash.

'The others in the society, did they have a say in this?'

'You will know soon enough if I stop looking after you.'

Another Lewis Doyle in my life.

'So, Dan Brown is my understudy?'

'Not everyone in the society wants you. We don't have to look far. Your previous lover, José Tarres for example.'

'What has Dan Brown to do with this?'

'Nothing. His interests here are not available to you.'

'Has he been here?'

'Why don't you ask your friend, Doctor Arnau?'

'Is it just your idea I take on this role?'

'You should be so lucky.' He took my hand and squeezed it hard until it hurt. 'Be on time tomorrow.'

He got off the sliding, noisy sofa and was gone. And then I had the answer. Of course, he got the idea from my books. He thought I knew more than I did.

Lewis Doyle called me from the US at 3.30 a.m. 'You'll have to pull the plug on this one. I've checked Gyp Planas. He is Central Intelligence and there's a NO GO on every line into him. Don't say too much on phone calls. He might have you under surveillance.'

'Why does he want me in this?'

'Someone with a lot of clout is behind him. It's their call.'

'Governmental?'

'I'd say, higher.'

And then I'd remembered the number. He waited while I found the napkin on which Gyp had written, '5521 years ago'.

'Yeah, Venus,' said Lewis. 'Beginning of the processional age. 3114 BC. Watch him, he's the one with the right numbers. Keep it nice and friendly with him.'

'Should I challenge him?'

'No point. It's the one behind him that's the problem.'

'Shall I just go?'

He paused, presumably thinking about him. 'I don't think there's anywhere to go to — now.'

Hadn't Gyp said something similar at the Casa Cundaro? And the room, although I was now in the familiar-facing original one, seemed too busy. The mirrors were the problem, too much reflection and energy.

Roca was at the door before the breakfast arrived and I thought his face was like a character on a Tarot card. He brought me bottles of water and fresh figs. His eyes were extraordinarily clear. Tokens from some other, almost changeless, state. I could see why Dali had liked him. I asked if he was only 39, as he had indicated earlier?

'What are numbers?'

'Everything, in this story.'

'Dali did the journey of the key,' he said. 'Some of the sites gave him such acute experiences, the only thing to do was to paint them. They were transforming in every way and took him into different spatial dimensions. He could go from three dimensions to eight, and become not visible to those around. He was reflected in the mirroring of the journey and saw endless selves and it drove him into an unbearable distraction that he could only, in the end, distort.'

So when the real got too much, it became surreal.

I realized you could only react to, and recognize the Cradle, if you were in an altered space. You couldn't just walk into Rebés and expect a transformation. The build-up of the journey allowed you that. Remembering some of Dali's painting, I thought I'd had better stay where I was.

Gyp was alone in the foyer sorting various photocopied documents. I told him we needed to talk about the secret, which must be a journey of reflected landscapes and significant sites, mostly historical, duplicated in Girona, the beginning of the journey and Rennes-le-Château, the end. 'Am I right?'

'No.'

'What is the point of the passing through this duplication, these mirroring experiences?' I asked.

'You are not listening. To know this, which was held by many before you, you have to be prepared and do the journey. Otherwise you understand nothing.'

The last sentence, one of José's, and I saw sometimes Gyp did slip over into a remark reminiscent of José. No amount of training obliterated that.

I reminded him I had taken the journey to the Portal, and he shook his head. 'That is entirely different. That is for beginners.' He sighed, and said he preferred talking to my secretary as her French was more understandable.

After a silence and then another, all wasting time, I told him he was giving me a role not his to give.

Silence over. His words, sharp and clear, 'You waste your time talking to Doctor Arnau. A custodian is a person in a job. He takes care of certain things. In his case, he carries out initiation. But he's on a payroll and he answers to his paymaster and maybe you should wonder who that is.'

I hadn't considered that before. He watched me, no doubt keeping the score. Gyp and Lucifer 100, Patrice 0.

So I included the threat of Lewis Doyle. If he started being too interested he would bring down the whole story, be bad for Girona and the rest of the material would be compromised. 'Girona, Gyp. We agreed we love this city.' It was the first time he noticeably listened to what I said. I gave him a quick CV of Lewis Doyle and he knew him or he did not. I added he had wide coverage.

155

'So, you listen to this person called Doyle or you listen to me? Which is it?'

If it came to something between Lew and Gyp, my money was on the latter.

'Do you really think I will let this person "take you down" as you say, take down the "shepherdess"? It will not happen. What do you think this man, whoever he is, can do to me?'

'Physically not a lot. Discredit, yes.'

'I worked for the CI. It will take me not even 30 minutes to find him, discredit him, finish him. So don't even concern yourself with things that are not important. Now, let's get your secretary and we will go to a special, almost unknown, place and you will see the secret takes care of itself.'

I wasn't getting up. 'So it didn't work with Dan Brown? He wasn't buying it?' Dan Brown had not bought it. That was why I was back, taking time. The little shepherdess instead of the mega seller. I got away from the slippery sofa and standing up asked the name of the society president or grand master.

He shook his head.

'Why should I not know?'

'Because the Masters are not named in their lifetime.'

'Lewis Doyle will bring down the whole story. He kicks shit out of fake.'

He got up, opportunities over. 'Let's go.' He went out to the car.

Piers called before I could follow and said he had done research on the Being of Light. It had appeared on the dates Gyp indicated and was called by different names according to tradition. The Celts called it 'Lug', for light. I asked if he could get information on life from that time. Unlikely. 5000 years ago? All traditions were passed from the Celts who came later. There was still nothing on the Stone Cradle. He said Lucifer was not a bad spirit. Ahriman was the satanic one. Lucifer was light. He was associated with Venus, but believed he originated from the East.

All I had to do was decide when to go to Rebés.

30

It had gone wrong before it even started because the prioress had gone to the other Benedictine convent of Montserrat, the famous one with the black Madonna. We would not be let in. We certainly would not see the special vault. This had been a firm appointment and I would not accept this cancellation. Each day, I lost money from my work in London and spent more, staying in Girona. I had to also give up taking care of my grandchildren. Why, when she knew I was coming, did the prioress not cancel it with Gyp?

'She did not know, then,' said Gyp.

I could see the elderly nun at the reception was truly hostile and I moved around in front of Gyp so I now faced her and said I was a friend of José Tarres, and he needed me to see the convent interior and the vault. At that name she smiled beatifically, and out came a torrent of Catalan in praise of my ex-lover.

'Mention who you like,' said Gyp, 'but it won't get you in.'

No way, was Gyp going to be let in. Maybe the number five was making him too invisible.

'Then let's call José.' I'd had worse ideas. The nun tried to look around me at Gyp. Somehow he had failed with this woman, and unbelievably she did not like him. 'Leave here or I call the police.'

'I am the police,' and shaking his head he went towards the car. It was then I realized he would have left me without a second thought. He needed the material José had withheld from him. I quickly selected what it might be. The end story – the Cradle. He had foraged along the frontier but he did not have it. I felt this was a very bad moment for Gyp that he kept whatever he struggled with under control. I got into the car and he said, '14 years of work gone in as many minutes and you did it.'

I took it he was talking to me and not some beam of light in darkness. Again, he pulled back into his training skills and stayed silent for the drive. Swinging up to the hotel, he reached over and opened the door for me to get out. I told him none of this was my doing and I needed to complete the work I was supposed to do. I had done my best to get a solution and reclaim lost time.

'Why did you have to mention Tarres?' He did not turn off the engine. 'Only the prioress knows about the vault. Only she deals with my entrances and exits. The nuns know nothing.'

'They do now,' the photographer said and I realized he was in the back.

'What's in the crypt, exactly?' I asked.

Gyp looked at me as though the next crypt I entered would be the final one for me. His mobile rang and, seeing the number, he answered immediately. 'No, it went badly. A terrible morning. I'll call you right back.' I felt, as I got out of the car, that the man who had called was the power behind him.

In the room, I asked Roca who the man could be. He did not know.

'Gyp must have someone important behind him. How else could he just go through Girona invisible with keys that open every door and go into convents and start lifting rugs looking for vaults? He's part of something,' said Roca.

Anna recovered enough to say it was my fault, and Gyp had told her I was not receptive. I could see the shepherdess role was hanging by a thread.

'And it wasn't a man he was talking to on the phone.'

'His wife?'

'His mother,' she said.

'How do you know?' asked Roca.

'If I don't know that I'd better give up my job.'

Throughout that unsettling day, my one solace was the recollection of the Blue Apples' site. Holding the Stone brought a confirmation of joy and that all would be well.

Lew Doyle called and told me to look for Lucifer. 'On the frontier there is a special stone, might be his third eye.'

'I didn't tell you about that.'

'No, but your researcher Piers did. He's 150 per cent on your side.'

I wished it was just the usual 100.

'We reached him, to get straight on this key business. You are doing good work. I'm right there behind you, sweetie.'

'That's just as it should be.' To be dreaded.

31

I stood holding the Blue Stone in Steiner House and explained
its passage of time. It had a new coating on the outside only 150
years old but the tile inside had enough weather damage and
other signs of ageing to be dated back to Roman times.

The traces of earth where the Stone had lain contained smears of
material much older, so the Stone had marked a place of possible
antiquity. Interestingly, the Stone, since being in London, had got
smaller, dryer and sad looking and both the stone worker and I
agreed on that and I should take it back.

The theme of the evening was, did the Magdalene reside in
Girona and did these Stones mark the graves of the descendants?
Lew was onto me immediately. 'Do they? I am tired of all this
dallying. I'm the one who supported you, so get off the fence.'

'Don't know.'

'Then I'm already there. I want graves, all interesting, with
artefacts and proof. I want to be up to my arse in grave shit or I'll
take the bastard down. After New Year in the States, I'll fly
straight there.'

That evening I contacted Gyp and told him that the inquisitor
was on his way to Girona. 'He wants to see the Blue Apples.' Gyp
paused and I asked if the descendants of the Magdalene and Jesus
were really there. I kept this devastating question that I never
thought I would ask, simple.

His voice lowered respectfully. 'I've told you.'

'This man means business, I've told you. Please let's defend
Girona from him. Do you have proof that the Blue Apples are
there?'

He said that was incontestable. He added he was happy to show
Lew Doyle the site any time. For once he sounded subdued. I said
we had three weeks.

For me the Blue Apple's site was valid because there was

something there, a joy that had just left, a sweet gentleness that could heal any scarred spirit. I was sure in my soul this was true.

My Catalan friend from the past, Lydia Arias, told me of Lluis Maria de Puig's death. She was his assistant in the government and had introduced us when I was researching *City of Secrets*. 'He mentioned you, just before he died.'

'Me?' I took a moment to absorb that. It seemed he had died several days ago in the government building.

'We had a big meeting in the morning and he'd flown in from Strasburg. I said, "How do you keep going?" He pointed to his coffee. He was going into his office to get some papers and suddenly stopped and asked about you. "Where is Patrice? Have you seen her? Where is she?" He hadn't mentioned you for years, not since the book. I said I hadn't seen you but as it was coming up for December would call before Christmas and give greetings. He went back into his room and the meeting was going to start and he suddenly rushed out and said in English, "Patrice is missing, Patrice is missing." He kept saying, missing. He went back to the room, became ill and died. These were the last words he spoke.'

I said the right things but I felt taken aback and completely mystified. Was it some energy that had brought me into his mind at what was soon to become his moment of departure? The psychic power Dr Arnau talked of? Should I have sent some healing for his distress? The thought put me in mind of the custodian role offer 'missing, I was missing'. What if, back in September the society had decided I should have the role and Gyp the guardian knew of it and decided to take me over, offer it to me himself, and quickly grab the society? It had felt all along like some sort of coup. Dr Arnau had not acted against Gyp and that was puzzling. I did finally call José and ask what the society would do.

'About?'

'Gyp.'

'Nothing. He will burn out. He is in darkness. The light always wins.'

Was de Puig, at that September meeting, possibly voting for my inclusion and now, approaching the end of his journey, he realized I was not included? 'She is missing.' It had to be that. I phoned Lydia and asked if de Puig was a member of a private Catalan society.

'Many societies. Amongst his documents is an envelope addressed to you.' I asked her to open it but she said legally she could not. I would have to collect the envelope.

I called Dr Arnau and he confirmed de Puig had been a society member. He added, material waiting for me would be useful for the journey to the key. I decided to definitely collect it. I thought gathering together a small group would deflect Lew. A group would keep everything safe. Soham and Piers said they would come.

I told Lew Doyle he would be one of the group.

'Group? Not a lot of losers?'

'Just one.'

I asked what did he expect from this visit? He wanted Blue Apples, proof, Usaries. 'It's big,' he said, 'bigger than you. It's not yours. But you get to write the book. We talk to Gyp and hear what he has to say. Then we buy him some drinks and hear it all again. I'm very nice until I'm not nice. He has to answer the questions.'

Not nice already, sweetie.

32

We were five at lunch in the Calle Forsa restaurant and the food wasn't good but this was not about pleasure. Gyp sat with photocopies of new information, including the Tablets of Moses leaving little room for the food. He said he had something serious and good to offer us and put a fork confidently into his cutlet of lamb. Piers was obviously pleased to be included in this private group and chose a delightful local wine to propose a toast. 'May this coming week be as delightful.'

Anna was prepared to do her best for now and took over the translation of Gyp's French, so Piers understood when necessary. Gyp's new man was not the mayor certainly and probably came from one of the municipal departments. The photographer was absent, so Gyp had to rely on this new friend to take photographs and he instructed him to stand and take a close-up of me, 'More lovely than ever.'

The friend stood up and lifted the camera awkwardly and I told him, sharply, to sit down. 'No photographs.' The friend, back in his chair, seemed sensitive and shy. I tried to set out what we should do most usefully in the time available before Doyle arrived. Gyp again claimed attention. He said the big surprise would be the opening of the Lazarus grave and he showed some images of what they had uncovered so far. It had never been touched. The owner of the building was an artist and he worked in a studio directly above the grave. Gyp had got permission to open this site and turned to the new friend who said a few words supporting the importance of the excavation. What the man did I wasn't sure. I found it difficult to understand him and didn't remember his name or why exactly he was there except to support Gyp. Piers said he worked in ecology.

Though a grave, this one of Lazarus wasn't the 16 Lewis Doyle expected. I cut in and told Gyp the inquisitor arrived that night,

Soham and her group the following day, and a friend of the guru sometime the following week. I no longer had any expectation of seeing the journey of secrets with Gyp and I was here to protect the Blue Apples' site and Girona from Lewis Doyle and collect the material de Puig had left and go to Rebés. I was very clear about what I was doing and how soon that would be thrown into disarray, I was going to find out. The saying, 'If you want to make God laugh tell him your plans' came quite suitably into my mind. I described the oncoming group to Gyp. They were all experienced adepts or academics because I wanted to make it clear I could, by my work, attract good groups and also protect my rights. I made it clear I did not need anything he was now offering because we had left, somewhat sadly, his original grand secret of 220 kilometres and I was back on Dr Arnau's original path.

He shook his head. 'Never forget that first day in Casa Cundaro and what I said to you. Think of those words. You are in it.' I dared to ask what exactly. 'If you are chosen but you are not a part of it you can walk away. If not —' He opened his arms. 'You work for an addiction charity so you understand that if you take one drink and are not an alcoholic you walk away. If the addiction is in you, you don't walk far. You take the hundred you didn't want. And that is a very simple example.'

'So the custodial role just activates something that is already within?'

'Exactly,' he said warmly. I had never seen him so softly and truly involved. 'So, do not dismiss the journey of 220 kilometres just yet.' And he changed the subject and turned to Piers.

What did he have on me? Was this a tactic to disturb me so I would give him information? The Cradle? The end story? What had seemed like a privilege was now a prison sentence. I cut in and said Lew needed to see the Blue Apples tomorrow as he only had three days. Did we have the documentation he had agreed we would, from the town hall? Gyp said the little-known man with us at the table was getting the permissions to cut the undergrowth.

'But it's cut,' said Anna. 'You can see the Blue Stones and that stretch of land clearly so someone has been maintaining it.'

'The paths,' said Gyp. 'Do you expect these people to go up the way you did, Anna?'

'Lewis Doyle, yes.'

'We are getting the access permissions and the name of the owner of that land by Wednesday.'

Every delay was always a Wednesday. I did not like any more Wednesdays. I said I meant proof the Magdalene had been there and the descendants buried on Mount O. We had agreed on the phone that Lewis Doyle wanted descendants and documents. Gyp showed no concern and I remembered Kathleen's words — 'Never underestimate that man'. And suddenly I felt such a stabbing pain for her loss — the death of Filip — I almost cried out.

Lew was another who didn't listen but he would listen to what came next at this table. He'd hear it, eyes wide open, kick shit, hours ahead. I was telling Gyp, Lew would expect lights and tools to open the graves.

'There are no graves, Patrice.'

'Your cat is dead, Patrice. Your book has failed. Your overdraft is refused. Your lover is married. This needs surgery.' His words joined that list. I wished I had the Blue Stone with me to hold, to link to that place of joy passing.

I remember only Piers's voice. 'Gyp doesn't understand. She means the tombs below the Blue Apples. Probably usaries.' Gyp couldn't have given the right answer because Piers quite clearly said, 'The burial place of the 16 descendants of Jesus and the Magdalene. Or is it 20?'

Gyp opened his arms to embrace a communal dismay. Was it sunny outside? It was dark in here. The room receded and I came back to the table. 'It's my work,' I said aloud. 'All down the pan. How's Dan Brown these days? You've not given it to him, have you?'

'No, Patrice. He's interested in Henri Croix.'

'The geologist from the Aude,' I said. He didn't expect that.

'Gyp hasn't given it to Dan Brown or none of us would be eating this food.' Were we? Anna had already passed on the main course. 'What outreach does Lew have?' she asked.

'A few thousand,' said Piers. 'And he's got some top people on his New York shows.'

He likes taking people down I said. 'He needs the power. That's why he sits on the fence, waiting.' I jumped around in the chair. 'Gyp, are there graves or not? When you say no, is it that they are not yet dug up?'

'Yes, that's what he means,' said Piers. He was becoming a tiresome optimist.

'They are under the earth,' I said, giving Gyp every chance. 'Undiscovered but too deep down.'

'There are no graves, Patrice.'

'Then you'd better start digging one.'

I would have left it and gone to Ripoll but I could not take Piers and he had come at his own expense to see the new sites for the research he was doing for potentially a new book.

I reminded Gyp of this and we went finally to the Church of St Roch to see the constellation of the Great Bear engraved in the stone above the church door. No one had ever discovered why it was there. It was centuries old and some said it had been imprinted by those from another sphere.

Piers talked with Gyp and the new friend about the Rose line, starting in Paris and the Mount O line, the Knights Templar treasure and showed he was not here for the Lew Doyle show but to do some work for my book for which he would be accredited.

'What are you going to call it?' asked the new friend.

'*The Stone Cradle*,' I said. And I watched Gyp's face and no amount of training could deal with that moment. He was drowning in dry air. Breathing was all done. He was done for. He looked for me, eyes finding mine. 'Save me.'

'That's a good title,' said Piers. 'You've never mentioned it.'

'Only on a Wednesday.' I was still looking at Gyp. 'Wednesdays are the days when I know what I have and what I do not have. What's your day, Gyp?'

He didn't answer.

'How about Sunday? That's today. Well, you always give me Wednesday.'

He turned and ran down to the car and he started driving before he even shut the door. We watched the taillight going off into the distance.

'That's smart,' Anna told me. 'How do we get back?'

'Where did you get *The Stone Cradle* from?' said Piers. 'We agreed there's no mention of it except in Turkey.'

I could see it was a cheap, quick fix, a retaliation that lasted only the shortest while and I'd have to live with the consequences. I had been upset and that's why I played the ace. I wanted to win because I felt Gyp so badly wanted me to lose. It was quite pleasant the four of us sitting in the dark on this winter night in the countryside. After a while Anna said he'd have to come back because he'd also left the local-government man and within the next minutes the car came quickly back to pick us up. I took him aside and said I could see the provisional title of the work had somehow disturbed him. I couldn't think why. It just seemed like a good title. I waited for his reaction. None.

'I did not rush away from you,' he told the group. 'I had an urgent text message and had to attend to it.' We walked down to the car.

'Why does *Stone Cradle* upset you, Gyp? Something you've heard before?'

'Nice try, Patrice.'

We stopped off to get hot drinks and I finally had to say something about what came next. Planes were crossing the dark sky and one carried the problem. What and how were we going to deal with Lewis Doyle?

'Introduce him to Dan Brown,' said Anna

'Don't tell him. Just say, it's a work in progress,' said Piers.

I knew that wouldn't work. 'You can't let him go up there, Gyp. If he sees there's nothing there, we're all sunk.'

For once Gyp agreed.

I phoned Xochi, the PR friend at Quest Publishers, from the hotel and she said maybe they wouldn't be allowed to dig there. These were graves and it would desecrate the land. Why hadn't I thought of that? She said the rumour was out that this was a serious site. If only Lew Doyle wasn't already so hooked on graveyards, coffins and corpses! And then I got a good idea. Let him dig the Lazarus one and then I fell into exhausted sleep.

Gyp and the men had smothered Lew with relics, designs, maps, diagrams, history and he was now a member of their group. They picked us up from the hotel covered with ropes, hard hats, axes, torches and Lew was excited. 'I'm onto something. Can't wait to see the Blue Apples.'

Gyp's eyes met mine and I was again sure he understood English.

'We'll have to do something,' said Piers, 'about the Blue Apples.'

'Hide them,' I said. And to Gyp, 'Why don't you show him the castle?'

He looked doubtful. 'That's not for sightseeing.'

I thought we could make an exception.

The Lazarus site next to the dark church of St Pilar was reached by a painter's studio on an upper floor and Gyp had already been there and set up the equipment. Passing an easel and an assortment of mediocre paintings we came, a group of six, to an opening through which the decaying chapel with the grave could be accessed. An adult could just squeeze through the gap. At my suggestion, Gyp agreed to let Lew be first in the grave. We set up enough cameras to satisfy an ego of any size. Gyp gave Lew goggles, gloves, attached a torch around his head. A near-bad moment, because of Lew's lack of height, was circumvented when Gyp replaced a man-sized safety vest with a boy's rubber-dinghy jacket. We stared down into the dismal area of the saint's tomb. There was a ten-foot drop onto the Stones. Was Lew up to it? Without his normal shoes, he did look shorter. This was his forte he said and ripped off his sweater.

Arms and torso, courtesy of the gym, were well muscled and he crawled forward, chose a secure rafter in the chapel roof, grabbed it, one hand, then another and to the surprise of the men swung himself into space directly above the grave. He had a choice of easing down the far wall or just letting go and drop. He weighed his chances and simply dropped the distance and landed expertly. I could now see the person who broke into churches, climbed towers, didn't bother with shop basements, only what was below. Gyp gave instructions of how to go under the floor level and into the grave. All we had to do, as a group was stay crowded in the tiny, talentless studio and watch, approve, applaud and photo-graph every microsecond.

Lew dived into the dirt of two thousand years and one arm appeared and held up a tarnished goblet. 'It's terrible in here,' he shouted, his mouth full of dust. He half appeared giving a mus-cular appearance and enough danger to make it interesting but was pulled back into the vacuous suck as the rattle and shove of stones he dislodged made a temporary space, one which he had better avoid or end up next to Lazarus.

Gyp leaned through the opening, prepared to jump and rescue him. He told him how to turn, what to grab, how to get free. Lew came into view, piece by piece, and the space he was just avoiding, filled up with an avalanche of stones and rubble. He got himself out and stood up covered with grave dirt and the men were fans for life. Now all he had to do was come back. He could simply open the door and walk up the stairs or climb like a spider up the wall. The wall won and shoving the goblet into his trousers he got himself up. The men pulled him the last distance and through the gap into the studio. Once again amongst us smelling of unknown centuries-old odours, we gave him our best compliments and Gyp now had an idea of who he was dealing with. The painter's wife suggested he wash himself and I gave him my bottle of water. Lew looked at me, half his face green and powdery, long-legged things hanging in his hair.

'Blue Apples next.'

Gyp looked at the goblet Lew had brought to us. 'I'll get a digger and some equipment and really get in there,' he said.

Lew did the grave scene once more at Joseph of Arimathea. I could see Piers and Anna had had enough of this male-bonding life-and-death challenging shit but could we leave this scene-stealer alone with Gyp? I think it was a kind of desperation that had Gyp stop at the castle and not easily step out in front of this rust-stained ruined building that seemed to stretch forever. He pointed at the Hapsburg crest and we stayed in a close group until the sudden wind subsided. Further along the wall 'Marie de Nègre's gravestone.'

The castle wall seemed too long with a dimension not unlike Jacob's ladder. Too much to take in, this building, that must not be mentioned according to my guide; not for sightseers as indicated by Gyp. It had been riven by terrible storms over the ages. People could pass it and never see it. Filip had said the nearer he got the farther it got. It was all about alignment apparently.

'I thought Marie de Nègre's grave was in Rennes?' Lew, quick off the mark.

'Of course. Duplicated. And here are the Tablets of Moses.'

This was safe. The men bent over these small stones on the ground and discussed them enough to appear to be interested.

'How about the Apples?' said Lew.

'How about lunch?' said Anna.

He didn't like it. So far he'd had all the attention he could possibly be given and we all needed a break. I suggested he went back to wash up and change his clothes. The graves were not guaranteed hygienic and the others including Soham, Holland and friends would go back for Manolo's three-course lunch. Lew did not like 'the others' but came with us as he was.

33

The tour of Gyp's diversions continued and I left them and went alone to Mount O. I climbed as far as I could and sat in a space amongst trees and concentrated on the Blue Stones somewhere above me and after some while I became warmed up and my breathing was no longer a desperate grab at life. I was in touch with a loveliness that allowed everything to be all right. And in its way I was free from time, just being there. I knew something lovely had come into the glade, a Being, a memory and the trees knew it and shook with the joy of it. I should leave but I could not leave. In that place Beings of beauty, sublime spirits had resided. And I knew I was right. And light and clear in myself I looked directly ahead and I had the impression I could see as far as the Stone Cradle.

Back in present life, the Lewis Show. Gyp presented the convent diversion. Lew had done enough graves and seen enough sacred geometry. He had kept quiet about the dubious key journey but he needed these Blue Apples. He didn't want another statue of the Pear. He was all through with pears. Done them in Perillos. 'Why are they stopping me?' he said. 'Is it you?' He was in a lousy mood. I started to walk away. 'I better see some graves otherwise I'll bring him down and everything with him. I want to stand in grave shit and know it's the right grave.'

'What if they're out of your reach?'

'If there is some bullshit, I'll take him down. That's what I do.'

'Why?'

'I enjoy it.' As an afterthought he said, 'And get rid of that fucking group. They're losers. Why do you hang out with these people?'

'You're in a group.'

'I am not in a fucking group of losers.'

'You're not privileged and different. What you see, they see.'

He rose up, cold and unpleasant. All the lying in graves hadn't done him any good at all.

'Gyp's guys all like me and would take me to the Blue Apples, anytime I want. But they seem to be nervous of you.'

'These ashram people are respectful and are my friends. I've let you come here as part of that. You're not on your own tour.'

'I see the Apples, then I'm out of here.'

'Then pay.'

I got into the car going to the convent and Holland would bring the rest. 'What are we going to do?' I asked Gyp.

'Show him the outside.'

'Not the convent. The Apples.' Then it occurred to me we couldn't get in the convent.

That night we ate in El Balco, one of the best and oldest restaurants in the area. It was Soham 's last evening and Gyp came to say goodbye bringing the shy, municipality guy in ecology. Lew sat opposite me with Gyp next to him as the centrepiece working out the duplicate sites on a scale of measurement, which now included Canigou and Rennes-le-Château and was beginning to resemble Liliane's map of the eleven sites in *The Portal*. Even Ripoll and Gombren were marked in. He was back to the old Gyp and these sites were his and his geometry was quick, accurate, and there was quite a discussion among the men. Lew said softly, 'I need those Apples, Gyp.'

Gyp answered, 'She's the custodian. You have to ask her.' He pointed to me.

I got up, the evening at an end and took Gyp off to one side. 'He's determined to go up there. He'll do it tomorrow .'

'He won't,' said Gyp. 'The only Blue Apples he'll see are the reflection of the blue balls from the windows of the hospital chapel if the light is on his side.'

As I was going out I saw a large, dark-haired woman wrapped in a shawl and I thought she was familiar. She had a blank face in which the features did not coordinate. I asked Holland what was wrong with the woman. Each piece of her face seemed too far from the rest.

172

'It's a plastic surgery job gone wrong.'

I asked him if he was sure.

'Sure. The flesh in between the eyes, nose and mouth is dead. It goes like that if you have a cheap job.'

I must never have a cheap job. And then I realized where I'd seen her — at the Antigua Bar in the rain, the woman with the face of stone.

In the night, I remembered something the Hungarian Kabbalist, Katy, had told me. It was shortly before she'd died. She said José has learned a way of restoring himself like Lazarus. They even called him Lazarus. He got the way of opening-up for spirit to come to him to heal and restore so he carries on his work. He is the true pathfinder. He's not afraid to die but he doesn't want to go yet.

Yes, he had pulled round from the heart attack, which changed my life and put me on the metaphysical route. He become quite transformed as Ani Williams said, 'A man filled with bits of light.'

Katy was present in his home when it was obvious he was very ill and an ambulance was called and rushed him, siren blaring towards Girona. She had followed with his son in the car but couldn't keep up. Then ahead they saw the ambulance had stopped and they got out thinking he had died. 'Imagine my surprise when the doors opened at the back and José came walking out just like always, light and free like the fool in the Tarot and I went after him because I thought he was a ghost. He said he'd asked for the spirit to help him, to come to him, to let him continue. "So I concentrate on the space in my etheric body," he said, "which I know how to do. And something glorious happened. I was made well. I will never forget to be filled with gratitude and bless each moment as it passes."'

I'd asked her what the light was.

Not what? Who? The Being of light, of course. The child in the Stone Cradle.

34

Gyp didn't come at 10.00 or at 10.45 and I knew they had taken Lew to Mount O and I was quite beside myself with an anxiety unusual even for me. It seemed to play into another time, an earlier epoch. Maybe some past where I had been betrayed.

Piers assured me it was impossible, as Gyp knew I had been protecting his interests and those of the city. It was clear I wanted to protect that sacred space.

The two cars pulled up at 10.50 and stopped further up than the hotel. I ran out into the street as Lew got out of Gyp's car and walked towards me. I looked at his boots. He had been up there. Mud, dirt and leaves, gave him away. Gyp came behind him smiling and it was as though his was another face and the smile was not his and it seemed as though he was coming from much further away and I'd been through this before and I saw no modern doorways, just the boots. Lew opened his hands in surrender. 'It's nothing. There's nothing there.'

And I could hear the voices of other men, too much male presence here, and I knew I had been betrayed. They'd sent Lew out first to defuse me. And I screamed at him. 'They will never forgive you!'

And I was talking about this time and another time. And the past seemed to open up like an old, heavy door but I could only see Gyp as a young man and I had told him the secret, which he vowed never to reveal. And I'd trusted him.

Probably had been in love with him and then he had appeared just like this, on this modern day. And he'd taken the men, the ones who should never ever know, to this place, and a tragedy followed. 'You have defiled what is divine!' I shouted. 'You are accursed!' But the sound was not heard in this present-day street.

I could see a past where I had told Gyp about the Beings from another place, another world. And he had taken the men to their site and these Beings, knowing only love, had welcomed them in and were brutally destroyed.

I sank onto a bench, only too much now in the present time. I would never tell the secret again. Dr Arnau came towards me smiling and held out his hands. I had no idea how long I had been sitting on the bench. He helped me up, no questions about the need for help, and obediently I walked with him to a large, cool car, its door open. I was encouraged into the back, its leather seats soothing and soft. He got in beside me and the driver drove smoothly towards the road for France. All of this without words.

Were they taking me to the insane asylum?

Dr Arnau put a large envelope into my lap. 'From our friend, de Puig.' I asked if Lew Doyle had gone.

'Yes, he's gone.'

'What will he do?'

'Nothing.' The nothing sounded absolute.

'It wasn't about the Magdalene,' I said.

'It never was.'

Dr Arnau sat, calm, not speaking, just there, not interfering with my distress and it felt right that he was simply there. After a while I understood, I was calm and wiped my tear-smeared face with a grimy hand. We got out in the countryside before Ripoll and he said, 'You have started the journey to the Stone Cradle.'

I asked where it was.

'Where the two circles overlap.'

The room was cool and shadowed with a stone floor, its pattern hypnotic, drawing my attention, allowing me to become disengaged from all turbulent thoughts.

'You've seen it before — the floor of the church in Rebés,' he said.

'I've been betrayed.'

He poured me more tea. 'Of course you have. What else did you expect?'

He sat watching me and I was glad he was in the world. 'What will Doyle do? He'll get back at me for this.' Gyp must be crazy to take him up there.

And I told him about Lew Doyle intruding on something divine and now he was cursed. The damage that has been done — he had aroused hate from another time. 'I am completely shaken as though there has been an earthquake inside me. I so dislike being so full of rage.'

'But it's been brought about by another's actions. He does the wrong thing and you are justifiably reacting to that. He's caused this anger in you.' He put his hand onto mine. 'You need to heal. Withdraw from him.'

'But he's gone, you said.'

'I meant Gyp.'

And I told him about the resurgence of another time and how those moments had taken over from the present. And it was not unlike a Portal experience. Past time could arrive suddenly and trip you up anytime on this kind of journey.

'I suggest you look at why you had to protect Gyp in the first place.'

'To protect my work.'

'Your books? And José as he once was.'

I supposed my earlier behaviour that day would once and for all put paid to the custodial role, whether it came from the society or Gyp.

He told me the reasons why I would be good in that role and I asked if he had made that decision the afternoon by the fountain. Had he not come to check me out? Intuitively pick up what I was about? He said it was more a meeting than a test. But the decision to ask me had been made by the society last September and de Puig was very keen on my inclusion. Dr Arnau agreed that was why he had said the mysterious words about my being missing before his death. I wondered how many other choices they'd had. He said I should practice the material in the envelope: the rituals, the meditation, and the healing of the past. 'Maybe now would be a good time for that,' he said, not without amusement.

'You will be invited to a meeting with some people just across

176

the border into France. There are certain practices and procedures necessary for this role. Your expenses will be paid. You have a daily time for meditation and the reaching of other levels of consciousness. You will be opened up and given more space for seeing.'

I asked how.

'We have a basis of certain numbers, certain patterns, depending on our birth and inherited aspects. This grid of numbers has to be changed.'

'How?'

'Aspects have to be cleared, speeded up in some cases.'

'Who are these people?'

'Excellent at transformation. Healers and Kabbalists. You will be sent the invitation and will be met at the airport in France. You can bring someone with you.'

I said I'd never heard of this before.

'It's called the Grid. And afterwards you will not tell what you know.' He looked at me quite firm now. I had probably done it in a past life, if past lives were what we thought they were.

'It is a secret that for all the money, love, power I will not tell.'

My granddaughter had once told me that, when she was six or seven but I didn't mention it to him. She was referring to the secret of the city.

'Why are you so angry with Lewis Doyle? He does what you would expect.' He almost laughed. 'It's Gyp Planas you should blame.'

'Why?'

'He took him there. And now you will meet one who comes to and from the time of those beloved Beings on Mount O.'

35

The woman stood in front of us, her eyes closed, moving from one foot to the other, turning an object from one hand to the other and with surprise I saw it was a piece of the Blue Stone from Mount O. She deepened her breathing, cleared her throat. I wasn't told her name and she turned out to be one of the best mediums around and I recognized with all of the adjusting to information from another reality, there would always be a margin for error. Whether the information came from spiritual beings, guides, guardian angels to which certain psychics had access, it would never be certain. It would often come from the wish to give good news.

She spoke English without an accent as she clung to the piece of stone. 'The spirit came through the atmosphere and the earth is wobbling. Into the woman's body he was born with the looks of a human child. The woman was here on Mount O and she was giving birth and suffered terribly. The child was handed to the group to be kept secret. The woman died.' Her face creased with pain. 'All around there is fear, people running, not knowing where to go. There is nowhere to go.' Her voice became dry and almost inaudible and Dr Arnau placed a glass of water near her. 'I can see a luminous Being of great beauty which seems to arise from the baby. I understand this Being of Light had to have a human body or the people around would have killed it. Yes, it's as though this Being comes from the child and holds the dying mother into his care — so much love for her and now the light's gone.' She shivered and moved the stone to and fro. 'They laid the baby in a special bed of stone because it wasn't a child in our sense. It had been born here with a magnificent spirit but linked with a much earlier time elsewhere.'

I had dozens of questions but had to keep them to myself. She was there, uncomfortable and present in this place and if I disturbed her she may go into shock and never get there again.

'I'm going back a long, long way.' And her voice dried up and she waited. 'This place, Mount O, is divine. There was a temple to the moon and the people were not from here: highly evolved, sublime, not from this planet. And they brought spiritual knowledge and intellect to the earth-born. And it is a wondrous place. And their light is still there. These Beings, so bright, brought gifts but the people were frightened of them because they were different and they killed them.' Her voice almost inaccessible she seemed gone from the room. 'This was one of the twelve places that God loved. Only four are left. And God loved these Beings.'

I am taken forwards, many thousands of years to the birth of the Being of Light on Mount O. 'He was brought to this earth to teach us, but one lesson had been learned from those Beings all those years ago. He had to go through the process of birth, to be in a human body and look as we do.'

I sat hardly breathing and I hoped she would not bring through anything terrifying and unacceptable.

'From Mount O, the temple hill, I see opposite, a little to the North-East. I can see a boulder and behind, a smooth dark-blue stone, cool to the touch. It is so smooth. I understand the child was laid there because it took sustenance from the stone. Nearby there is an opening in a mountain to other existences light years away. A Portal, but in those times, open.'

She opened her eyes and Dr Arnau offered her the water, which she did not seem to notice. She pressed the stone to her forehead. 'The cradle-child was from elsewhere and the arrival of its spirit here was terrible. The planet shook and there were storms and spectacular change to the atmosphere and violent winds, every-thing black. People running to and fro, terrified, not knowing where to hide. They thought the sun was crashing into the earth. Then everything was suddenly still and dark, and the child was finally born on this hill to a human woman. Lights appeared in the sky that had not been there before. And the child was laid on stone and brought in a new and wonderful era. A woman came from the East to look after him, to rock the cradle. He was a great teacher and brought a new consciousness to these people. He walked from place to place from the cradle to the temple near the mountain hill where he was born and he brought healing and passed on the rituals. He lifted the people to a level of intuitive knowing. He was in Egypt during the construction of the first pyramid just over five thousand years ago.' Her voice became warmer and stronger. 'He was love, knowing, communication, one-to-another without words. He created a place of learning, a school. Today his light is still here in traces. It leaves the earth slowly and the traces can be held and made strong. He has left the light for us.'

She paused for a long time. 'He was not Jesus. He came 3000 years earlier, the Light Bringer and today there are people who keep the light, like carrying a torch down the ages. They light the pathway from the Stone Cradle to elsewhere.' She seemed to go back to some other time and her voice changed. 'Other people came to Mount O and took over the temple and made it theirs. The temple is always to worship the moon.' She straightened up and wanted to open her eyes but they were kept shut as though held. 'It has always been known only to a few. Years ago they kept it secret by turning it into a pleasure garden for people to sit in the evening, drink water from the well or to dance and play ball-games. But it was a disguise for what was there. There are some who move around in that area who appear as human beings as we expect them.' She paused and drank some water. 'The female who came from the East is still around here and there. They call her the Lady with the Cup. She heals.'

She put the stone down, her eyes opened. 'This stone is not old but marks the place of the temple of those sublime Beings. It is the earth around it that is old. José knows this but will never tell.'

Later I tried to ask her questions but she did not want to be taken into this again and said I should definitely not go there. I could be a caretaker and that was all. Who gave birth there? Was she sure it wasn't the Magdalene? Now out of trance, she did not know. Only it had to be kept secret or the child was at risk. But the Magdalene came later and was nothing to do with the earlier Beings. Would Magdalene lay her child on a cradle of stone? She said she was amazed how old Mount O was. I asked her where the cradle was and she said north. I said, 'Do you want to come there?'

Dryly she replied. 'I've just been there, haven't I?'

Before going back to London I did have the chance for another talk with Dr Arnau and I asked him what he thought of the words of the psychic and could he confirm them.

'Some.'

'How do we know this story?'

'By oral tradition down the centuries. Some by deciphering the designs on ritual rocks or stones. Some scrolls. But always through seers in the temples and through people such as that psychic. And other ways.' But he didn't elaborate on what they were.

I said I was curious about the word 'school'.

'It was said he began schools here and in Egypt.'

I asked the name of this Being of Light.

'It depends on the tradition. Some call him Lucifer. The Celts who would have been the first to write the story, called him Lug. The shoemakers' guild Luz—light. He was the Bearer of Light.' The woman from the East? I said Xochi and others said Lucifer came from the East.

'A female or goddess came from the East to nurture the child,' he said.

'So, it was here?'

'Here. And he used the circles.' He paused. 'They were from a time long before.' Another pause. 'Let's go more slowly, one journey at a time.'

What was it he did not want me to know?

36

Away from the ever-reaching tendrils of the past I got back to work in the neutral energy of London and my life was practical and structured and suited me. I phoned and asked Dr Arnau, if Girona was the lock, what then was the key? He told me to draw the circles overlapping the Cradle site and draw a line from Girona to Rennes with Canigou in the mid point as I had with *The Portal*: Rennes, Girona, two towers, two altarpieces. 'You have already been told the journey is made up of circles. Work out and draw the lock then the key and send it to me.'

What was duplicated in the two sites, Girona and Rennes? Piers and I made a list and I asked Dr Arnau if Gyp's material was valid. 'Only where it has already been established. Remember the points you have been shown over the years. He has not included all those. Then link them starting with the Barraca, One, French Garden, Two, as de Puig's papers indicate. I'm afraid you have to do the work.'

Was I preparing a book or a custodial role? He allowed a pause. 'Go on with the material and that will become clear.'

'Why am I chosen?'

'Chosen? Let's say offered. You are a sensitive, a medium. You are creative and you do service by healing and working on addiction in the community. I am sure you have been told you are an old soul. You care for children, look after them.'

'They're grown up.'

'You look after your grandchildren.'

How did he know? 'If I can, of course.' What had this to do with the custodial role?

'You still look after these children and others.' I thought he'd hung up. 'Remember what I suggested about Lewis Doyle. Never forget who took him there.'

I listed those sites shown to me by Liliane and José and I

checked with the material from de Puig and could see a fountain or a well accompanied each one. Whoever had drawn the material numbered the sites in the order they should be visited, as had Liliane in *The Portal*. They did not include Gyp's hospital chapel, the Star of David, St Roche. Linking up what I had with lines, gave the shape of a young bear, like the drawing of the journey in *The Portal*, but sharper and thinner. As before it corresponded to the constellation of the Great Bear and the seven stars. Girona and the province came under its influence. How did the key from Rennes look? I was told it wasn't like a doorkey. Was it a shape or energies, ideas or intentions? José was the keyholder and opened the lock. To other times, other realities?

Piers had duplications of Mount O, Girona in the flowery mountain at the church of Rennes. There were similarities in the painting opposite the altar with Mount O.

The altarpiece of Magdalene corresponded with the tomb of Joseph. Then I got another page of the de Puig material translated and read it more carefully and thought I understood we had to have a talisman in here. The oriental cradling the new moon?

I made no contact with Gyp. I supposed, as always, I closed the door on a bad episode and went on to the next good one as I always had. Suburbs in London? Get out to Hollywood. Marriage break? Hollywood. Bad luck? Out dancing. Shock? New lover, fame, excitement, originality. Down? Couldn't spell the word. So I didn't overthink the Gyp/Lew betrayal but got busy with the research and Cradle practices. Girona wasn't metaphysical in the Glastonbury, Rennes-le-Château sense. It was mystical.

But when I got the invitation to go to the Grid at the end of March I was reluctant and then I realized the dark time in early January had not been resolved. It didn't just go to Hollywood. I trusted my friend Wendy, a healer in London, and always went to her with the big stuff.

'You want safety, lately, and you won't get it on this. But it's a privilege and what you've been preparing for all these years.'

Anna and I flew into Nice to stay with a friend and we'd make our own way to the Grid meeting-point with a woman from Aix.

We stayed up in the hills near St Paul de Vence and there was snow in the mountains and the air was fresh and a delight to breathe. I could rest my heart just looking at the lemon trees, the oranges, the land, bountiful and rich. It was the end of March.

After two days when we were due to travel onto the Grid people, the plans were changed. A car and driver waited outside my friend's house. It was a Prius Hybrid and the woman, blonde, in her 30s, said she would now take over. She took the motorway to Aix, the car eating up the miles. After Fayence she went right into the backways till we reached Brignoles.

It took just under two hours and she spoke about alchemy and how she wanted everyone she came in contact with, to have a better time, a happier hour — change the dark through to the light. 'I can help them do that. It's alchemy.' And she made these simple comments positive and I felt cheered up. Then she was silent for some while and I asked if she knew Dr Arnau. She said she was French, not Catalan, that she had not seen him, but he was a celebrated man in the true sense.

We stopped on the motorway for a coffee and water and she showed me an exercise to drop tension. I sure needed that. Then she said she'd met Liliane and all tension vanished at that name. It would all be all right. I tried to ask more about the destination and what I could expect and she said all that would be explained to me. Where were we going? Just a small hamlet. She found out Anna was in the shrink trade and she'd met a couple of A-list practitioners and that interested Anna and so all attention was off me and my unanswerable questions. There was no news of José. Maybe he was not on this earth anymore but I was sure I would know of that.

Intuitively I would receive that news. Then something else occurred to me. What if they needed to keep him alive — even if he wasn't? Would the society do that? I decided in their favour. They could.

The last location I noted was the small town of Brignoles and then we were into the country and there was a signpost but she sped past that, another at an intersection but I didn't recall any names. I asked where we were.

'Almost there.'

'No. The name?'

We cut through one hamlet, then another. 'Incognito Street,' she said in English. She was an excellent driver, calm and smooth and we crossed into a narrow lane and slowed, reaching another hamlet with a knot of houses, a church, a shop, a bar and no name. Another kilometre and into a private property. There were no neighbours, no sound of passing traffic, just birds.

She parked the car and took us quickly through a simple back door with a porch and crossed through a kitchen, a simple dining room, along a clean shining passage. Everything was clean, bright and non-descript. Any housewife, anywhere in the world who knew her stuff could produce this. I recalled garlic and onions hanging in the kitchen. It was the house of a peasant. She led us into a workroom with a desk and chairs around the walls, a treatment bench, a photocopy machine on a side table. On the desk were pens, a block of A4 notepaper and a ruler. The walls were covered with pictures of saints, and in the middle an image of Jesus, which I thought was from a shroud. The place was simple, tidy, scrupulously clean. It had no personality. There was not one suggestion of class or comfort or luxury to be seen. Outside the garden door boxes and tubs of plants and herbs, a mangle. Through to another room, books from floor to ceiling, neat and arranged in cases. Sound of water and from the other window I saw a small fountain. Yet the atmosphere was light and hopeful and I would have said good things happen in this room.

Anna was looking at the items on the desk. 'It reminds me of a family-run healing business in Lourdes,' she said. Since when had she been in one of those?

'Don't leave me,' I warned her. Nothing here remotely linked with the society, the academics and luminaries of the past. And then I thought that they had brought me to the wrong place.

The man came in swiftly, wearing a vest and baggy trousers and if he had had braces they would have been hanging down. He was maybe 70 and from the South and was a peasant until you looked into his eyes. They were discerning and far seeing. He hugged the driver and they agreed this was a beautiful day. He spoke French and told Anna to sit to one side and I in front of his desk. He was full of energy and life and this man would walk and plant and play boules and sing until you saw the eyes. They belonged to exceptional places. He said it would turn cold again and we should all be aware the spring would be the extension of winter. The woman should wait in the kitchen or go for a walk. She could make a drink or whatever she needed.

Anna took over in French and introduced me, a friend of the custodian, a friend of José Tarres — yes, yes, he knew all that. He shook my hand, then hers and his name sounded like Alice but it was Aless, an old French country-name that I would never be able to pronounce. He sat opposite me, took a pen and notepaper and asked my mother's date of birth and her maiden name. Problem. I didn't know it. He took that in his stride and I asked why he needed it and he didn't reply. I gave her details as they had been given to me. He seemed to have photographs of me taken at different locations and ages. Had he been rubbing shoulders with Gyp? I said the name Gyp Planas and asked if he knew him.

'I know many people, but in the end, do I know them?' He looked at Anna and laughed. She joined in. To me he said, 'This is what you will come to understand.' He got to work humming or singing as he did so, quick as a little bird, head one side then another, his bright eyes black and shining sharp. He wrote my date of birth in numbers, then my mother's and added them up. Then he crossed some out and arrived at new ones. He drew symbols, triangles, circles, very fast. He drew three charts and worked out complex configurations of letters to which numbers were added or erased. Numbers there, then they weren't. He did a scale of mathematics like a music score ending in a sum that satisfied him and he blew out his breath.

Another sheet and he changed my name and it became a string of letters. He drew all this expertly, quick, whistling through his teeth, and ended with three copies of a sheet of Kabbalist signs. He selected a recent photograph, taken from behind, and entered dots along my spine and shoulders in a cross. This was photocopied several times. More circles around my head and shoulders and he asked for my passport. He folded the three charts into small pouches and attached one in my passport, behind the photograph. 'Your new identity. Voilà.'

The bigger one had writing across my forehead and heart but he kept that. The last was a photocopy of my back with the cross of dots and he said to keep it under my mattress, always facing north. My name was back and there was a tower in ink underneath.

The work took an hour.

'You are now freed up. You were born a medium, have always been, and will now have the vision of a being alive here in 2091.'

'My God,' I said, horrified.

'You are speeded up, expanded and we will work on you.' All I could think of was, if I died could I get rid of this?

'You have a connection directly,' he pointed up, 'to Thuban.'

I asked, 'What have you done?'

He laughed loud. 'She still questions and she has all the answers.'

He took another sheet of paper off the block and drew circles of identical children and he put me in each one. 'I have given you a place here.' He showed me but kept the sheet. 'Remember it.'

We'd been in the room one hour and a half and Anna had sat still on her chair near me. I hadn't noticed while watching him that the room had filled up with men and they sat in a line along the far wall. Aless pointed to my chart and asked Anna to translate, 'We will keep you in good order.'

I asked how.

'By heightening the levels. You are looked after. They—' he pointed to the men, 'will look after you. Going through Portals will be like going on tube trains.'

'Where do you get this from?' said Anna.

He pointed to the wall, but by mistake I looked in the mirror and it reflected a figure I thought I recognized—the woman holding the crescent moon. As soon as I spoke the mirror filled with reflective objects on the opposite wall. I said I had just seen a talisman. He nodded absently.

'All from over there.' He pointed up.

I was then placed on a stool and moved around side to side, forward then back, lastly far down and I didn't like that. He lifted me up and I asked why he did this. He said my left ear had stones sticking to the hairs, which affected my balance. He didn't think much of my knees and moved them unusually. I could feel the heat of healing on my head.

And then he stopped, and that was that, and we were free to go. I did try to ask about the talisman and looked back at the mirror. He spoke quickly, 'Remember you are a seer. You can see into distances, future, past. You've had the brakes on. You will always be tested. You are a sensitive being—chosen.'

Back in the kitchen, and the woman got us into the car. She sped out of there through the place with no name towards Brignoles. She made it clear she wasn't able to answer questions. She only knew they did miraculous things in that place.

She stopped in the centre of Brignoles and said we could get a coach to the airport. We weren't going to an airport but back to Nice. She could not possibly take us back. She was now late. I couldn't believe it. I said something would always go contrary to any good that was happening.

Anna leapt out of the car and tried for a taxi. Could we phone our friend in Colle-sur-Loup? No trains, no buses, one taxi and Anna said the driver was psychotic. Anna was furious and I panicking. Somewhere in all this, a beautiful young Muslim boy was there in a car beside ours, a gang of boys, mostly black and Asian, with dogs gathered around him. The boy spoke to the blonde driver and said he would get a car and take us wherever we wanted. The woman told Anna he would do it and to give him a few euros.

'I don't need euros,' he said. He got out of the car and leaned into the window to speak to me. 'I know you are scared but I will get you where you need to be.' His voice was unbelievably gentle.

I wasn't having it. He was too young, probably didn't have a licence; he was dealing drugs; he was on drugs; his car was stolen.

Anna said we were in a real problem and were stuck in this place. He was the only solution. She turned to him and said to get the car. She was rough with the blonde driver and the boy looked at me with extraordinary loving eyes, like Roca's. 'You will be all right with me. Remember it's a test.'

I didn't get it at the time.

He drew up in a very smart vehicle indeed.

'I told you it was nicked. You got me into this,' I tried to blame Anna.

The boy got out and held the door for me. He had a lovely, soothing voice. 'What is there not to trust?' he said. The rough boys and rougher dogs bumped around the car. Anna got in beside him at the front.

'The nearest town,' she said. 'A hotel.'

'Shall I take you to Aix?'

She had another angry exchange with the woman and the boy drove sweetly onto the motorway.

'Is this your car?' I doubted it.

'Yes, my father bought it for me when I passed my exams.'

I asked him how old he was and he laughed. 'Old enough.'

'You have a licence?'

He got it from his pocket and handed it to me. He was Arab. Aged 18.

It was only after skirting Marseilles I realized we were going south to Montpellier. 'This isn't the way to Aix,' said Anna. 'Can't you read?'

'Why Aix, when you should go to Spain?'

And then I understood what I almost did in the turmoil at Brignoles. I was being tested. This was a continuation of the Grid. The scene with the blonde driver? Part of the test. How did I do? Poor. Was he in on it? I asked him but he said he didn't know what I meant. He saw two ladies in trouble and wanted to help. He said he did not know the blonde woman.

Anna said we would sleep at a hotel and she would give him

189

money. By the look of the car he didn't need what we could give. They, the Grid men, wanted to see how I coped with strain and the unexpected. It was all so like Liliane's work on the journey to the Portal. You got to know yourself or you didn't make it.

The boy stopped as we came into Avignon. We'd been on the road some time and it was almost dark. I said I had to clean up, eat, and go to bed. We stopped at a restaurant opposite the Hotel Europe where I'd stayed a few times when my play was on during the festival. The food was fresh and beautifully done and I had soup and carpaccio with fresh figs and then a local fish dish of the region. We all ate with pleasure and I remembered that he drank only water and was calm and good to be with. He said his name, Rami, and he was at university, studying science. Afterwards we walked along the river and said we'd get a hotel here.

'I think we should keep on the road. Where you need to go is not to sleep.' He looked at his watch. 'It's not even ten.'

'Where did they tell you to take us?' I asked.

'No one tells me. We should drive.'

'Where do I need to go?'

'We'll get there.'

As it was getting light I could see a crossroads and looked quickly for a signpost. He continued tirelessly along this secondary road and then I saw a turning with a sign for Rebés. I told him to stop and he said he hadn't seen it and wanted to keep going. We were deep in the country, nothing on the roads and I said he must turn round and go back. 'This is the middle of nowhere,' he said. 'But the light is beautiful.'

He did a U-turn and we joined the sliver of road for Rebés.

Through the still-sleeping village to the sloping hill, open on all sides, the mound high enough to give a good view of the sky. He stopped the car near the graves and walked up to the fountain. He said it still worked and offered me some water. The chapel, the school, the country house, the public telephone, all as it was, lit by the clear, uninterrupted dawn light. A touch of a chilled breeze made the trees shake. Then I heard it. The sound of sweeping and it sounded good. I walked to the place of the Stone Cradle and there was a courtyard in front of the dwelling and a woman was sweeping with a generous old-style broom. She was thin, small, with long dark clothes and something on her head, tied up like a scarf. She looked at me and carried on sweeping. Yes, it was a pleasing sound. There was still dirt on the courtyard and a sprinkling of dead leaves and she swept faster getting the brush one way then another into the corners. She straightened up and could be of any age. She looked out at the horizon with its rim of silver.

'It's the best time, isn't it? The beginning of the light.'

I said I wasn't usually up at dawn and as it was this beautiful I should do it more often. I wanted to look at the Blue Stone Cradle and wondered if I should just go there or ask her. She offered me the broom and I saw she was old and I got up and swept the central space just for the pleasure of it. I said, 'Who will do this?' I meant the sweeping.

She replied, 'The children will take over.'

And then I could hear children and they were laughing and talking on their way to the school and it seemed like a lot of children for a small place like this.

'They go to school so early,' I said.

'Oh, these children have already been to school.'

I would do anything, just about, to live in this moment. I don't know peace like this very often. Was it peace or deep serenity provided by the atmosphere of the place? And then I realized the children had passed by and weren't going to the small school on this hill. I swept the far edge of the courtyard and Mount Canigou was suddenly just there, up the road. I hadn't realized it was so near. There was nothing between us and it. The peak was pink.

'The children will be here?' I said. Hoping they would look after her.

'There will come a moment when they have had enough. They will be caretakers of this place.'

'What, here?' I was trying to get it straight. 'Just this place?' She could see I was thinking too parochially.

'Everything.'

'Who will run it?'

She was a surprising person.'They will.'

'On their own?'

'They will be helped from elsewhere. You should read the prophecy of the society.'

She took back the broom and stood it against the wall.

'All societies have prophecies.'

I walked to the Blue Stone and she followed me with her shoe-flapping walk and lit a long white taper. As she rocked the long elegant stone, I asked her how it had got there.

This is a dream! Wake up!

As I walked away I noticed her shoes were familiar, and they looked as though they were from the East. From the hill, I saw the circles forming, huge in the silver light and I was sure there was movement and small figures converging, children gathering around the rim.

'You'll come back,' and she waved to me.

Wake up!

Luckily I remembered the way forward and found the car. Later I realized the woman was Asian. Her shoes were like those of the figure carrying the crescent moon.

37

As soon as I arrived in London, Piers and I started the research. It was biting cold and we went to Lemonia for lunch. This was the cold the Grid Master had predicted. Anna joined us and that's when the misunderstanding started. Piers had asked if our flight was held up by the sudden snow. She said Aless had promised the winter would come back. He asked who that was and she realized she'd said enough. 'Just a friend in St Paul.'

'It was okay by train,' I said.

'We took the plane,' she replied. 'From Aix.'

I promised her we had not, and she felt in her pocket. 'Well, I wouldn't have the boarding pass but I've got the ticket purchase slip.' She couldn't find it and I felt quite frightened for her. Was all the strangeness and metaphysical mystery getting too much? I was sure she had been in the car at the back sleeping. I said I'd talk about it later. I was also worried the strain of her work and all this travel was catching up.

When Piers left we walked on to Primrose Hill and I asked gently if she felt any different after visiting Aless.

'None,' she said briskly. 'You don't have to change your entire journey because you want to keep it from Piers. He doesn't care.'

So I said the ride to Rebés had been a surprise.

'Sure is,' she said. 'We took the plane back from Aix.'

'The next day?' A qualm now. Not yet panic.

She couldn't be bothered with this and made a phone call. I asked her before she left for Oxford what plane we had taken? 'Ryanair, Stansted, last flight.'

So where had I been for twelve hours plus? It was like some drug-alcohol-induced blackout. Yet it was all clear and so easy to recall.

'You do remember the ride with the boy?' I asked.

'The taxi driver, yes.'

'The quarrel in the town?' I'd even forgotten its name.

'We got a taxi to the airport. The woman had driven us to Brignoles and we nearly missed the plane.'

There were no other repercussions and these were enough and I carried on working in London.

Except every creditor I'd ever had, and even ones that had forgotten I'd owed them anything, were on my doorstep or phone. And I actually couldn't believe it. From years back. There couldn't be anymore. There were.

I did feel out of balance and the healer I'd always gone to said it was a reaction to the Grid change. I'd told her about most of it. She said I'd been speeded up too much.

Why?

'So you can reach spiritual beings, and they you.'

'What beings?'

She hesitated. 'Like the ones who reach to assist with your healings or come through when you tune in psychically for people here. Like them, but further away. These men sound as though they are Kabbalists. You are not a young woman. They should think about that but they are men. They want you spiritually enlarged and activated faster. But what about your poor body? They have tuned you up too high.'

Alarmed I now told her everything.

I called Dr Arnau and said I hadn't heard from Lew Doyle. Neither had I seen any outcome from his visit to the Blue Apples. I had said he wanted to reveal it as fake. I dreaded his reaction, as it happened.

'I told you that is what he does. That's all. It's his job. Remember who took him there.'

I hadn't heard about him either.

The only other affect was when I told a shiatsu massage friend about the numbers and Grid being changed and she had heard of something like it. She and her husband came through the snow and winds of March to hold onto me physically as they filled in their lottery numbers. They even did some coupons for me. They paid out real money because they couldn't lose. A writer, with psychic tendencies, with a Grid change and new numbers, was unbeatable. We even had a slight problem of who kept the tickets because did we really believe that person would not be tempted to keep the money? The result was unthinkable. The only number that came up was eight.

I was called back to Girona in the first week of April. Dr Arnau accepted the key and lock, which Piers had drawn, using a large-scale map of Girona. The lock was formed by the sites in Girona in the shape of the thin bear under the constellation of the Great Bear and its key was represented by three duplicated sites in Rennes and they were drawn at the top to the north-west. Together the lock and key unlocked the circles, which accessed the journey and were overlapping. We marked a line between Girona and Rennes with its Caniguo centre point.

Dr Arnau pushed it back to me. 'Now, turn it around so Girona is the key and Rennes-le-Château the lock.'

I asked why.

Landscape with view of Canigou – the sacred mountain of the Catalans. Winds here reach over 170 kms, but the cradle site was nevertheless built in its path

'We deal in duplication with this. Now all you have to do is the journey.' I assumed he was joking and after a little laugh admitted the drawing was complicated.

'Not really,' he said. 'The ones that include the celestial links and constellations are a challenge and require sacred geometry.'

'So there are energies from other realms out there?' What a novice. How simple could I be? Even a woman's mag horoscope had familiarity, at least, with the names.

'So you will start on the journey?'

'By car?'

'You build up power at each point. You go from the Barraca to the French woman's house to St Lazarus to Mount O and then you go round the circles in a figure of eight. You notice, Rennes is included as you use these three sites. You stop there and you circle back to the Cradle. The key and lock are then completed. It is open.' He didn't say anymore so I asked, opened by who? 'You will tell me. The lock and its key is the small opening. The big opening is overlapping circles. You may experience, as you move around the circles, images that Dali witnessed.'

How I hoped not.

'You will learn to accommodate that.'

How I hoped so. I asked if I was linked with a planet or star or energy beyond our earth. He said I'd been told when my Grid was changed – Thuban.

'What do I have to do?'

'All the sites of the journey, from the lock to key to Cradle, are surrounded with energies. Some have become knotted up, like tangled knitting yarn. They have to be untangled and cleared. By energy. And some of this knotting up has hardened like barbed wire. We have to cleanse and heal. Some of the vibrations of these sites reach a higher intensity, over eighteen thousand units, so only an initiate can be present in this sublime force. A person who has not got a level of initiation can become unhinged, paranoid, but occasionally, illuminated.'

'Who do I go with?'

'Go with?'

So he was one of those men my healer did not like. Was his care all surface? 'I can't walk that distance.'

He laughed and touched my face sweetly. 'Come on, I'll take you.'

We would walk some of the way but mostly he would drive from Girona to Rennes and around the circles. He believed I had already started the journey and some of this would be easy and quick. We would go in May. In the meantime, I was to work on the meditations and rituals. Especially those relating to the journey after death. The only one I liked was the rocking one — forward, back, side-to-side like a cradle.

As I left his house I saw a circle of children in his garden singing and holding hands. It made me think of Rebés. 'What are they doing?'

'Being children.'

I turned and asked for the truth. The prophecy. Was this planet going to be taken over by children?

'I hope so,' he said. 'They can't do a worse job than we have.'

'When?'

'When the overlapping circles eclipse and become one. Children are being prepared now. Think how fast they grow up. Many are psychic, Indigo children. Think of your granddaughter. She is an example.'

Had I mentioned my granddaughter? 'But she's eleven.'

'It was she who gave you the idea for the title *City of Secrets*.'

'Yes.' Had I ever mentioned that in the book interviews?

'Tell me exactly.'

'We were in a taxi going down Baker Street in London and we passed Sherlock Holmes museum and I said, "He was a famous detective, real only in books." She said, "Every city has a secret, and for all the money, love and power, I would not wish to have." I didn't know whether to write what she said down before I forgot it or ask from where this had come. I scribbled it fast and said, "Where did you get that?" I was quite calm, she was seven. She said it had just come into her mind, but every city had a secret. Didn't I know that?'

Dr Arnau was silent and then he said the prophecy was bright and optimistic and we should be glad about the children and learn from them.

I told Soham about the children. I told her about the visit to Rebés. I did not mention its name. I told her about the talisman with the oriental being holding a crescent moon. I mentioned Gyp as the dark force, the military, the overpowering and José as the light, the healing, the poetical. And then I said it was from another place, all of it. It was a pre-arranged script from another source, not earthly.

Soham didn't find anything I said alarming. She felt they were using me to prepare for the rituals. She had heard an accredited scientist in the States predict that the people who took over this planet would be young. She would look into it for me.

On my next call to Dr Arnau I asked if the men in the place that had no name were tightening the Grid so I was going faster. It was too fast. He said they would only balance me so I mentioned the discrepancy in the journey home, Anna on a plane and me in Rebés. I felt he breathed in deeply.

'You have been expanded. Your consciousness. Your dream state. Your receptivity. You will make journeys in the etheric realm, as do most adepts to begin with. Visionaries do this.'

Oh God, the last thing I wanted. I said I wanted it all reduced. Just back to normal, like Hollywood normal.

'It may be uncomfortable to begin with.'

I began to understand why José didn't want me in this.

'Just write the book,' he said. 'We will do the journey when you are ready.'

'I will keep calling you.'

'Fine,' he said.

The atrocity in the US, yet another where a guy with a gun went into a school and killed and injured so many children, made me think of the Asian figure in Rebés. 'They have had enough.' I felt, yes, they would have had enough of this. Of the constant assaults on their beautiful spirits, why would they not rise up and say it's enough? I wondered who they were, the ones from elsewhere. I hoped they came quickly. We needed them.

38

I came into the room in the Girona hotel and the flowers in the vases shivered but there was no draft. A little reminder from another place, nothing more. Doctor Arnau phoned and asked if I'd seen Gyp. Not at all.

I was driven towards the frontier by two men who worked for Doctor Arnau. By the roadside a small group of men were peering into a hollow. 'He went too near.'

'Too near?' I asked.

'What they call the vortex on the mountain. You can't see it but it sucks you up.' He was a local farmer and pointed to Canigou. 'It's invisible,' he continued.

'The Portal,' I replied.

Doctor Arnau took me to one side and so taking away more chance of conversation. 'He went too near. That is the verdict.' He said the energies were very low around that site to protect it. Human beings are not welcome. You can't be there for too long or you're weakened. 'This man,' he pointed across to what I assumed was a ditch, 'he had no protection.' He held me back from joining the knot of men, some standing, others bent over, what I took to be the corpse.

'Is it —?' I was going to ask if it was someone I knew.

'It's not clear,' he said.

'I'd like to see —' I wanted to be sure.

The thing was like a grey paperclip pulled out of shape. The body had been electrocuted to a point of non-existence, and lay twisted, shrivelled, metallic grey, the clothes still smoking. I allowed myself one look.

'It happened no more than an hour ago,' said the farmer.

I thought I recognized Pepe, one of Gyp's men in the group, and I asked what had happened. He said the voltage had been extremely high but it wasn't clear from where.

'What was he doing there?' I said. I realized although I was as rigid as a statue with shock, my tears fell liberally, obscuring everything.

'Is it his shoes?' whispered Doctor Arnau.

I wiped my eyes and it took a moment to see where the shoes were exactly. The saving feature in all this was the burned corpse was unrecognizable as a human being. The shoes were strangely untouched, and I thought, too expensive. 'He didn't walk in the forest. Not with those.' I looked at the mountain to steady myself. It wasn't clear if it was Gyp. Some person, unknown to us, could have walked here and been struck by lightning.

'Is it his shoes?' said Doctor Arnau, urging me to look again. And then I realized something I should have noticed immediately. Gyp was sturdy and big. Those shoes were not his. They were too small. And Gyp would never go too near anything, let alone a Portal.

'It's not him,' I told the men.

Pepe was consoling, but firm. 'It is Gyp. He must have been up there.' He pointed upwards at the mountain. 'He's been missing for some days.' Looking into my eyes now, he said, 'It is Gyp. What is he doing there? He should never have let the American on Mt. O.'

We waited, a desultory group, for the police and forensic people, their sirens screaming in the distance. One look back at what was in the ditch. The clothes had been singed beyond recognition. The one eyeball hung by chords to a socket that was no longer there. 'It could be anyone,' I told the men.

Doctor Arnau bent down and detached a shoe, enough to see inside. He scratched at the heel. The cars pulled up and we were asked to stand back. They touched their hats in greeting to Doctor Arnau and called him Sir. He was still occupied freeing something from the shoe.

'So you thought it was me, little shepherdess.' I turned stricken, expecting at minimum, a ghost. Gyp in full flesh and definitely alive had soft footed taken a place beside me.

'You look surprised to see me.' His eyes stayed on mine, taking

200

no chances, making sure whose side I was on. Satisfied, he said it was a shocking sight, and I should rest.

He bent forward and touched the dead man's shoe with his foot gently. 'Electrocuted.'

'It could be anyone,' I said.

'Yes,' said Doctor Arnau, 'but in this case it's Lewis Doyle.' And he held out the piece he had extracted from the shoe. 'It's a shoe lift. Not many people wear those.' He just didn't look at Gyp.

'He was very keen on graves,' said Gyp. 'Always attracted to those. But we don't need to bury him.' And he pointed down, 'He's already in a grave.'

And in all directions were small burial signs, broken or sinking, headstones, a cross, it's message obscured, an urn, half visible.

'It's the old cemetery outside Rebés, unused for years,' said Gyp. 'I wonder what he was up to here.'

While the men sorted out the official details, I sat on a gravestone, my attention always coming back to the mountain. It was decided Lewis had most likely died trying to locate the Portal. I felt desolate that we should end up with the small attachments we had spent our lives gaining, protecting, lying broken and exposed around us. We finish up, identified by a small secret-aid to being good enough, in his case the shoe lifts.

I could see why Lewis would want to challenge the mountain, get its secret, maybe be its friend. I remembered my arrival at the frontier with Beryl all those years ago, and how the police pointed at the peak. 'That's the Portal. Takes you to other places.' Maybe Lewis, his spirit, had gone to one of those.

The police chief wanted to question me, and Gyp said he would translate. First I asked if there was any chance it could be a man taking a country walk that morning. 'No chance,' said Gyp. 'We've confirmed the dust on his shoes. He's been up there at the peak.'

They wanted to know all about Lewis. The trouble with the metaphysical world, you knew nothing about anyone.

Gyp said he would take me back to Girona and save Doctor Arnau the petrol. If they had spoken together throughout the investigation, I hadn't seen it. I felt too exhausted by all that had happened and simply could not go anywhere. I needed to phone Xochi and people in New York and let them know what had happened. I wanted the easiest safest option, and said I should go with the custodian.

'Not so fast, shepherdess. I know you do have feelings for others and you do care.' He obviously meant for himself. 'I'm going to return the favour. Do not trust everything that looks smooth and well mannered.' His eyes moved to where Doctor Arnau was waiting in the car. 'Those people can be dangerous. So I'm going to show you something. It's another sort of journey.' I said I'd do it, but for now I'd get into Dr Arnau's waiting car. I'd got just a touch of 'danger'.

They said in the press an unknown man had been struck by lightning. They didn't mention there had been no storm. It was their best interpretation.

39

The vast mountain, majestic, absolute, was unusually accessible with no shadings of weather or camouflage of light to create atmospheres or promote mystery. From summit to base, it was brilliantly lit by the strong sun, and challenged to give up its secrets, its crimes. It was too present, and the light only brought it nearer to our frail, only too human group. It was innocent with no relation to our misfortunes. I could hear Liliane's voice. 'But, of course, you have to let go. Do you think anything is yours? What do you own?' Not much, as it happened. She'd shown me that on our journey under the constellation of the Great Bear at the site of acceptance.

I looked for news of Lewis Doyle on social media, and I asked some of the metaphysical groups he frequented. Not one mention of his death or disappearance. Xochi tried his contacts in New York but they had been told he'd gone to Egypt. I suggested she reach his family. 'Did he have a family?' she asked. Was his name Lewis Doyle? Dr Arnau confirmed the deceased body had been formally registered, but there were no identifiable possessions visible after the manner he met his death.

'It's up to his family or close friends to make enquiries.'

What if it wasn't Lewis Doyle in that old grave? Whoever it was, twisted over like a paperclip, had been violently electrocuted. It occurred to me it was not caused by lightning, but more an atomic blast. Then it occurred to me, maybe Lewis Doyle had simply disappeared because he needed to.

The sky was exceptionally blue, deep and rich from an exotic part of the world I did not know. I asked for a taxi and a woman answered the call. I asked to go to the place of the Stone Cradle and she had no problem with the destination. She had blonde hair, tied back neatly, and a confident driving manner, and turned up a hill at the end of town, as I would expect. I asked if she knew the Stone Cradle. She said, 'Where else were we going?' There were still houses in this quite noisy area but I seemed to recognize the place. She stopped as I expected, but not at the exact destination, and I pointed to a house further along.

'I am not going there.'

I pointed again, and I said I knew it was the right one.

'No taxi would ever go there.'

'But it's there, I need to go.'

Was this another deceptive blonde female driver? I asked what was wrong with the house. In the blue light it looked mysterious and a little shady, as though things went on there – gambling, opium, parties and music. There would be a lot of that. I said I would pay her more if she would go there. She wasn't having it and said this place where she'd stopped was much better.

'You are sure of a good time here. You're with our sort of people,' she said.

I had no choice but to leave and she turned round back down the hill to where I was staying.

I paid her and went inside the hotel which had glass doors and through them I could see she stayed parked outside. Another taxi was about to pass. She called to the driver and he slowed to acknowledge her. I hurried outside and told him directly that she wouldn't go to my destination. The woman leaned nearer to him and said, 'She wants to go to that place. You know the one. The Stone Cradle.'

'Oh, no,' he said. 'We can't go there.'

'Why not?'

He gestured for me to come closer and he kept his voice down.

'Things happen in that place.'

'Please tell me. I need to know.' I held onto his door.

'Something happens to the people who try and take it over. It doesn't end good. The last one who owned it –' He shook his head.

'Prison?' I asked.

'Mental home.' He was about to drive off, then put his head

close to mine. 'The ones who really own it don't come from round here.' And he looked at me and thought I'd got the message.

And the blue got too bright, and I woke up and knew it was a dream, hoped it was. It scorched my mind, rocked me absolutely.

40

It was spring, the time of the flower exhibition and I suddenly wanted to be in Girona. Not for the flowers or the fact it was spring. I wanted to see José again. Change 'want' for 'had to absolutely'. Just one last time. And then I understood I could not be there alone. Was it because Dr Arnau had proposed a journey to the Cradle in May and yet had still not come up with a date? This was May and I should take some control over the outcome of this custodial decision. I should get on with what had been suggested. In or out, it must be my decision. I phoned him several times but his answerphone gave no information. I understood he was often away. Cynthia suggested we call it a visit and keep the group small.

Masia was laughing and over the years the laugh had got merrier. 'Men with machines have been cutting the brambles on Mount O so Gyp made a path for the shepherdess.' Maybe it was the memory of that ill-advised visit to the Stones the preceding January but I couldn't bear to hear Gyp's name. I believed it was this accursed action that was responsible for Lewis Doyle's death. I hadn't been in touch with Gyp nor he with me since that time. I asked where he was now. 'Nowhere to be seen.' I also asked about José.

'As always sunny and bright but he's a poet. But Gyp has done something crazy even for him. He's cut the undergrowth around the Blue Stones. He got his friends in the municipality to do it. He thought it belonged to the municipality. It's privately owned and they are furious.' He laughed more. I asked who owned it but he didn't know.

'You remember telling me that Gyp wanted to build another tower in the French garden?' Masia nodded. 'And someone stopped him.'

'They did.'

206

'It was José,' I said

'Yes. Because he has the power. That's what started all the trouble between them. This was last May and Gyp was jealous of José. He found a way to get back at him. You. And he would take over the society.'

'Could he have done?'

'Yes,' said Masia. 'He has the police and politicians on his side. They want to change the society and get the power.'

'But José won?'

'He will always win.'

I couldn't find the Cradle site in Rebés yet I'd been there a month ago. I had to raise my game. Anna hired a car and we drove to Rebés and found the small 'family dining room' where we had had lunch, José, me and the men some years before. The owners were the same as I recalled, perhaps less disagreeable. In French, Anna asked the directions to the deserted hamlet and the owner said he'd never heard of it. He was one who disliked her excellent French and said in French he spoke only Catalan. If she wanted to speak French the border was 20 miles away.

I told her again, the site was on the small track to a hill to the south.

We took the car along the track I remembered and we should park it by the gravestones. She'd gone the wrong way because we ended in someone's private land in which stood a restored country house. We took another better road back to the eating-place and started again. There was a hill but it wasn't that hill, so back to the village and we asked questions. We chose the old villagers and described the chapel and the school.

'Oh, the place of the skull.' The man continued with a warning in an untranslatable dialect.

'But where is it?'

He waved his hands. 'Anywhere.' And he didn't want to talk about it further.

We went back to the first hill. I climbed the slight mound on which the refurbished house stood in good grounds.

'It's been done up,' said Anna. 'Good views.'

We walked to and fro and I had to give up. And we started back to the car and I saw the fountain. I crouched beside it and she had to ask if I was all right. 'It's been built on. It's gone.' So where was the small, stone house with the Cradle? Whichever way I walked I could no longer find it. It was as though I was in a spinning vortex, forced to continue the same tightening circling path which avoided my choice of direction altogether. I did see a smooth stone just lying as though abandoned on the hill, dusty and broken at one side. It was slightly hollowed out in its middle. Would they just leave it open to the sky, to the casual gaze of a passer-by? Didn't they do that with the matching landscape? I tried to rock the stone and was greatly relieved when it did not move.

They said in the village a local man had rebuilt the house. They didn't know anything about abandoned buildings. Except the baker's daughter who remembered originally it was a strange place.

'And he can't seem to sell this done-up house. So now it's up for let but no one stays.'

Gyp was too quiet. Would he simply let me go into the control of Dr Arnau and the society? Gyp with hopes dashed was a dangerous thought so I sent him a message and was relieved when I received an email, 'You are the most disobedient of all. From the one who loves you best, little shepherdess.'

I knew I was followed, could feel it, couldn't do anything about it. Even Luis at the Arc said it would happen. 'I don't know what the society is but I know what they do. Remember my father's death? It is better to go mad then to go around sane knowing things they'd prefer you didn't. It is not a small matter.' He leaned across the bar to speak softer.

'It has to do with some other system. It's not controlled from here. Just think, people have seen the vision of the Lady with the Cup. Does she come from here? It has to do with the planetary system. It's not controlled in the usual way.'

These words still resounding in my thoughts as I left the bar, made me unaware someone called my name. Then Gyp pulled up in his car quite friendly and said I looked well. I had expected at least some serious discussion. Did he not remember Lew Doyle and his death? Did he have amnesia as well as no ingoing lines and an impossible ego? Thoughts came quickly these days. The Grid men had done a good job. I should be ahead of the game and let the enemy follow. I smiled at him, all Blue Apples' betrayal forgiven. We were just two people getting through things, this life and a dozen previous ones. I did remember his words. We were in this and could not get free. I did feel a sort of kinship with him. I suggested we drive somewhere and he was all for it. I thought of the one place he always avoided. 'Let's go to the castle.' Did he know I was trying him out?

He hesitated. 'There's nothing to see. It was a military fort.' He was unwilling but I got into the car. 'It is not for you. It's not a settled place.'

Ah, so we were getting close.

'The winds are terrible there. The storms are ferocious.' I assured him this was a sunny day and so start driving. 'Storms just come from anywhere in that region.'

I said we should live dangerously.

I found an opening in the castle wall and was amazed at the vastness of space behind and the number of buildings almost intact. This was the hospital. This the keep. Here the barracks. He said for many years, arms were hidden here to stop the French.

Philip, the Hapsburg king, built this castle in 1604.

I noticed he kept his voice down and he almost crept from one building to the next making little noise.

'What's here, Gyp?'

'Just memories.'

I almost passed the dilapidated building which the sunlight made beautiful and I could see through the broken arch to something on the back wall. I could make out drawings of constellations and a cluster of sacred symbols. He pulled me away. 'Not for you.' I waited while he climbed the broken remains of a

209

bell tower and went back to what I had half seen in the shadow. He was behind me with exceptional speed. 'Not there.'

I asked why not.

'They buried their dead here.'

'They?'

'The immigrants,' he sounded unwilling.

'Immigrants? Where from?'

'They stayed here.'

'When?'

He chose the 50s. I didn't believe him.

'From Spain you mean?' Helping him out now.

'From Spain, yes.'

'The poor from the south, Gyp?'

'Running from Franco,' he said, more assured. The dictator was always a good excuse.

I doubted that. No one would run into Catalonia in those days. The Catalans were trying to get out. Franco hated the province, targeted the people from all sides. They were killed, imprisoned, simply lost. The dictator's grey police arrived in the night in 'blind cars', cars without lights and the ones they picked up were often not seen again. You didn't simply come from safer parts of Spain to that environment to find money, work and shelter.

In another building I could see paintings in the gloom. Graffiti? It looked better than that. I tried to get closer. They weren't paintings but maps, beautifully designed. Not maps in the usual sense. I wanted to go in. He would not. Why?

'Bad luck.' He couldn't wait to get back into the car. I stayed where I was. 'Tell me what happened to Doyle.' I sat on the wall and refused to move. I tried another question. 'Do you believe in the descendants of Magdalene and Jesus?' He stopped a little distance away and kept his voice down.

'What do you think?'

'No.'

He shrugged. 'Well, maybe it's something else.'

'Something else definitely, so why say the Stones on Mount O are to mark the descendants of Jesus?'

'A lot of people these days believe it.'

'So why say it's true?'

He moved forward serious now, not to be fooled with. 'Those Stones mark the existence of something phenomenal, so be careful. I am on your side.'

'I didn't think you'd killed Doyle.'

I had. I'd cursed him.

'I hoped it was lightning.'

He wouldn't sit down and again prepared to leave, car keys rattling. 'It came from another place like an atomic blast.' He stopped and would have stayed stopped.

'Why are you in it? You said both you and I could never be free. What did it mean?'

'Just that.'

'How did it happen?'

'I feel you're a poker player. So am I. Let's have a game one night with the guys. Everything else is too late.'

I waited for Masia to open his shop and I asked about the castle. 'Immigrants there at one time?'

He looked wistful, hoping to return to those prudent days when 'I've never heard of that' said it all.

'Gyp told me to ask you.'

'At one time, years ago there were strangers and their children up there.'

'Why?'

'Presumably they had nowhere to live. They had a lot of children. And they must have moved on somewhere else.'

'What sort of strangers?'

'I never saw them. This was hundreds of years ago before my time.'

'They did amazing pictures and drawings,' I said.

He was enthusiastic. 'Yes, the maps, other world.'

Other world, the Stone Cradle, those children. Why not? 'Were they from Spain?' He decided on an answer.

'No. They didn't speak. They moved away. They were a colony so I'm told. It's only a legend.'

'Gypsies?'

That idea cheered him up and set him free. 'Probably.'

'They weren't Gypsies, Ramon. They were the Stone Cradle children.'

'Never heard of that.' No longer cheered up.

41

Rebes is a wild place and not for human beings. A vast area of prehistoric rock and stone and gnarled, remarkable, still existing trees. Dolmens, other druid and pre-druid sites and an occasional building isolated up a track impossible to pass. Signs, warning of every kind of danger, made these tracks uninviting.

'That olive tree. Stop.' Soham got out of the vehicle and felt the trunk. 'This is very old. The oldest I've come across.'

Holland pushed through the impenetrable growth. 'That one there. Real old.' She couldn't reach it and Sundance suggested she get back in the vehicle. 'What's the hurry?' she laughed.

What was the hurry? We were all on edge. This was not an area of certainty. Soham had never seen vegetation that old and the stones and roots and trunks all twisted with age, not part of our lives. There was absolutely no relation with us and Holland used the word we had each considered but not spoken. 'Alien.'

'It doesn't belong to us,' said the Spaniard with wonderful hands who understood stones.

'And doesn't like us,' said the German girl.

Eight of them had brought me here to find conclusively this hamlet I'd described on top of the slope which must exist as it had been seen in late March and had not become a refurbished dwelling as I'd thought two days before. We had driven in circles and not found it. Mario the Gypsy violinist was going to play somewhere on this inhospitable land to call up the spirits. After this drive we changed it to 'appease the spirits'. We bumped and jolted over what should be a path for vehicles and my back was now out and the others covered in bites and stings and only Soham remained unscathed. Overwhelmed by the strangeness and atmosphere of this landscape we again sank into silence.

Sometime later we were suddenly out of this strangling

experience onto a swathe of land surrounded by mountains and high hills and in one corner huddled against a hillside the substantial remains of an extraordinary monastery. The light above and piercing through the mountains was as clear as the first ever light. Beside a sharp pointed peak the usual patch of blue light I associated with this place. Canigou was almost in sight. I said the hamlet I was looking for was near. Mario with his violin hurried to the monastery and climbed high up the side and this was impressive for a man not used to climbing. Holland took the drum and followed and they quickly sat on a jutting piece of the wall and played music. It was more than that. It was a calling out to the spirit of the place to come, to befriend, to join us. The violin pulled up the spirit of the land and called to one who was missing. Sundance shivered and the eight of us stood transfixed and the patch of blue sky became ever more pure and the music soared to the sky and a swirling, whirling movement of dust, like a corkscrew, spun towards us growing bigger and continued on over and up to the violinist and it sped and spun around him and then off to the mountains. It was one moment we would not forget and we had momentarily joined with the spirits of the place and we had made this connection ourselves by our action. Mario and Holland came down from the wall, eyes shining and wild with the senses of the place.

'You called up the dust,' said Soham.

'Oh, yes,' said Mario. 'I saw it coming towards me and it reached my hand and I had to struggle to keep the bow on the strings.'

We got back into the vehicle all quicker than we would have liked but there was a sense of get-out, this is not ours. And yet it was so magnificent and remote.

'I feel I'm being watched,' said Holland. 'Everything I do is seen.'

'I agree,' said Soham and others agreed.

'This is a vast moonscape. What could you do here?' said Sundance.

Again we argued as to where the hamlet had been and by agreement we did not mention the Stone Cradle.

'Everything is deserted. What happened here?' And the German girl began to cry.

Holland at the wheel seemed compelled to suddenly drive up a slope, rocks rattling, stones spitting, scraping metal, stalling, jolting, dogs howling and around the tight bend. Unwise, but he had no fear and as a reward he arrived at a country house.

'I hope they don't shoot us,' and he got out. A wiry fast-moving man with dark hair tied back came forward. He had a sensitive, finely drawn face. He was academic, professional and was a surprise in this place. His movements were lithe and assured — and he showed no concern. Speaking English he agreed we had made a special journey to arrive at his house.

'I keep the road unattractive so no one much comes up here.' And then he saw me — and I him — and it was a meeting of energy and recognition. Our life journeys had arrived at this point and crossed — and I knew he was in the society.

The guardian of the Cradle? The rituals? It didn't take much to know that.

I explained what we were looking for and he said we had passed it several times. 'In Rebés the energy isn't as elsewhere. Energy is in circles so people get lost.'

'Sounds about right,' said Holland.

'We just want to know the place she is looking for exists,' said Sundance, ever to the point.

'I understand your question and why you ask it. It should not exist because no one would build a hamlet on top of a hill. Everything here is constructed according to the wind from the mountains which can average 120 kilometres. You cannot live in the path of this wind — or you are destroyed.'

'So who built it?' said Sundance.

'No one from here.'

'So what is it now?' Sundance was too full of questions and this man, he turned out to be a lawyer, was not going to answer.

'In Rebés everything is built away from the wind. The monastery is sheltered as I am. I hear it. I am not in it. The place you mention is deserted.' He was looking at me. 'Men shooting in the woods have taken it over. They have covered one of the build-ings – perhaps to disguise its identity. That way, with the guns, the site is protected. No one goes there.'

I understood and nodded. The protection was simple and worked. He looked at Sundance. So it cannot be approached.

At that moment we heard rifle-fire and dogs barking.

Holland tried to turn the car around.

'Better to back down,' the man said.

'I can't do that little journey,' I assured him. My spine – rigid with pain yet to come – I asked if he would walk me down to the track and he was happy to do that.

'One minute,' said Sundance, 'where exactly is the site?'

The man pointed in the direction of the monastery. 'Past the house of the olives.' He took my hand to traverse the sharp bend and I asked if he was here permanently. He worked in Barcelona during the week.

Above us Holland started the descent and I heard Sundance say, 'That man is covering up.' I hoped the lawyer hadn't heard it. Holland pulled down the last incline – and we moved to the side.

'Who would live here?' I asked.

He laughed. 'Only another adept.' He looked at me, amused.

'But people know about this place.' I was thinking about Gyp. Did he?

'Possibly. They come to measure the energy. Then they go away.'

'Do they find anything?'

'Only that they can't find anything. I am pleased, at last, to meet you.'

'Likewise.' I loved his smile. I asked his name. He shook my hand.

'Kim Carreras. Yes, I am his grandson. The priest who looked after the cradle.'

Holland straightened up the vehicle, and I asked quickly what the lawyer did here. 'I assumed you were creative.'

'I restore the chapel of the Cradle and that in itself is a creation. Next time I will take you up to the hamlet.'

216

And for a moment I remembered it. It was higher than I had thought with an amazing sweep down to the sea. A bell had tolled in the wind. I remembered the swinging door. Holland beside him now shaking hands.

Sundance asked who had built the hamlet.

'No one from here. The approval did not come from the municipality of Rebés. It's desolate. Unliveable. No human being would think to build anything there.'

I told him people would always look for it.

'They won't find anything. After all, you have enough trouble finding it.'

Driving fast Holland reached the village. He added, 'I'm glad to get out of there. I don't know where I have been—but it isn't Rebés.'

Mount O took away time. Time could no longer exist as it did down the hill below. The Blue Stones were in a straight line across the hill, above us the ruined church dedicated to the moon. It was a place full of a joy that had just passed and you could sit and walk here and experience states of being unlike any other and all good. It was a blessed place. The Gaudi hut was wonderfully made but broken, the tiled floor the same as the floor of the Lucia tower. It was light and happy, a place to which you could always return physically or by thought.

Was it Dr Arnau's linking with the past that made me feel the presence of those sublime beings; all love, all trust? They welcomed us. We were accepted.

I met Masia in a cafe and asked what would happen to the Blue Stones' site.

'They will be as before. Overgrown. Not known.'

I said I wanted it to be as it was once: restored to a place of pleasure, light hearted with lamps in the trees, music, healing and meditation.

'You could,' he said thoughtfully. 'It would cost money.'

When I didn't object he said I should speak to Dr Arnau and hurried back to his shop.

I couldn't wait to go back to Mount O but at that moment someone was beside me and thinking it was the waiter I asked for a mint tea.

'You want to watch that university boffin, Dr Arnau. Well, our accounts are due now, have to be drawn up.' Gyp leaned towards me. 'He can't help you there, little shepherdess.'

I didn't get up Mount O that afternoon.

42

The room was spinning with photographs and the noise jarring across every nerve. But this was not the Casa Cundaro. The room was stone, old and too big.

'But it's the castle, Patrice.'

I had, as a card-playing friend said, 'Crapped in my own nest.' I had seen the woman with the face like stone as she'd left the Café Antigua. I saw she'd forgotten an object on the table. It turned out to be a small Stone Cradle. Following her brought me to the castle. She was Gyp's mother.

Gyp moved closer to me leaning across the table. The photographs around the walls were of stones, dolmens, figures from previous centuries and graves.

'I am still offering you a gift. Last time it was to be custodian. Now it's to get out of here and go back to your hotel. Just point out on the wall the Stone Cradle.'

I would not get out of there, even if I did recognize it amongst the dozens of stones spinning into the distance and back again, on this mighty weather-damaged Hapsburg wall. As far as I could tell we were alone but then the mother rustled in with her long skirt and shawl saying it was far too hot and she gave him a bowl of cold water. She wetted a cloth and put it over his forehead.

'José is not going to save you, even if he could. I am not afraid of dying. Are you?' Terrified as it happened but not telling him. He pointed to a photograph, not a stone, but José and me years ago by the sea. 'Puerto de la Selva—'68,' he said.

'You must be quite deep in, Gyp, with all this José stuff. Jealous. Seems like it. You even sound like him sometimes but you can't be José.'

His time not to answer.

'You said we are in this, you and I and we can't escape. It's in us.'

'Correct.'

Was I in the story? This one? Or the past? Had I, all those centuries ago, played a foolish role? I'd told too much. It would not happen again. 'We betrayed something then. Is that why we are locked into this past?' I looked at him.

'Sometimes I think so. It's just a glimpse. I don't know. Then the thought dissolves.'

'But you said it's in you and it's in me.'

He said this heavy heat had given him a headache and put the cloth back into the water and doused his face. 'I nearly reached the end because of it.' He sounded softer and his eyes as they looked into mine were pained and for a moment I thought he needed me. 'I get no peace. There is no rest.'

And I remembered what Cathy had said about getting his orders from a beam of light in darkness. I hoped that was all it was.

'The graves and Stones called to me, give me no peace. "Come here, Gyp. The secret. Over here. Try here, Gyp. Come to us." ' His eyes vulnerable. The eyes of a child. I realized he was looking at me for help. Should I speak? Should I not speak? 'And I think sometimes the best is to go to those graves.'

'Where did it start, Gyp?'

'At the frontier. I was on patrol and the communications went down. No signal. Just static. And then this noise, not of this world and I saw this ray of light. Unusual activity passes through there. It interferes with reception. We always thought it was because of the mountain. Some nights there was so much activity you could not get any signal or contact with the men. It became a flare of light filling the sky. And then I knew it was there, the Cradle, so I chose to patrol the frontier.'

I sat as soft as butter letting him talk, needing him to talk. Then I would be free. All the time his eyes were soft and he showed emotion, I would be free.

'It comes from a shaft a long way away and tells me what I should do. Every night. "Come on, Gyp. Do this, look for that." There have been times when I have wanted to die. I have seriously considered that option. They won't leave me alone.'

So I asked who they were and he shook his head.

'No one would believe it. Only a crazy would go for that.'

I took his hand and wiped his eyes. 'We can tell them to go away.'

He let go of my hand. 'The men decided the ray of light made night day and we waited for the explosion that would come. No explosion. I didn't know if all the men were all right. We decided it was just a chemical charge from the mountains. The men forgot about it but it didn't forget about me. It's the same occurrence that killed Doyle.'

A pause now. Should I fill it? Carefully I suggested he tell the voices from the graves to stop. 'You can,' I said, absolutely sure.

He tightened up, good move over. I had not understood.

He got up and turned on more machines and I understood he was familiar with the castle. It was his workplace.

'I've looked for the Cradle for 30 years. I want it and I want it, now.'

'You're new to the game, Gyp. I've been looking all my life.'

'And you've found it.' He put a sheet of paper and a pen in front of me. 'Just the name.'

'I can take you there.'

'No, Patrice. Trust, as you say, is not our thing.'

And then the woman brushing the courtyard came into my mind. She was the Grand Master. It belonged to other Beings than us.

'There is a problem, Gyp. You remember you said Dr Arnau is only the custodian? And I should ask who owns the society?'

Got him. He didn't know. But he wasn't going to like the answer.

'Don't try and say José or the woman who sits up at the ashram.' He re-wet his cloth and put it over his head.

'I wouldn't say that, Gyp. The owner knows me. You have to activate the circle and go there in an altered state or you will see nothing. They don't come from around here.'

He grabbed a professional looking light, with wet hands, plugged it in the switch and turned it on so the beam pierced my face. And I held my piece of Blue Stone from Mount O and my hand was sweating. He put a thumb gently on the paper. 'Write the name!'

It came from nowhere as I picked up the pen. A dazzling sheet of lightning, like an explosion blasting everything into darkness. And I heard the woman scream, 'the plugs'.

The electricity and the equipment blew, blowing the plugs and there was a smell of burning and then the terrifying thunder shook the building. It was clear Gyp had been struck or electrocuted. He tried with all his might to reach out for me, 'I just want to protect you, little shepherdess. You don't know what—' I thought he said—'they will do.'

I was out of there, through the gap in a newly broken wall, running like hell downwards on legs that had not run for years and through the lines of houses, praying and the rain like daggers after me and hailstones fell like plates.

And more lightning flared enough to show the city below and I laughed and I used to be frightened of lightning.

43

The sweet-faced lawyer, Kim, turned the well-used Land Rover fast around the narrow track. No waiting in Rebés. The vehicle, accustomed to rough rides, bounced over every obstacle, and I reached for the seat belt.

'You don't need that with me.' And I was attracted by his quiet power.

Although the track was barely suitable for one vehicle, he did not decrease his speed and seemed totally confident he would not meet another conveyance coming the other way. Kim was 42, a man of the soil and spent three days a week at his law practice in Barcelona. He told me this in a calm practical manner to get my mind off everything else. The vehicle's interior was designed for work on the land, lacking any niceties. The seats were worn, the back filled with sacks of grain but the engine would be well maintained and never let him down. He had money enough and didn't need to show it. Boards attached to trees along the track warned of danger. Others – 'NO ENTRY', 'HUNTING IN AREA – BEWARE SHOOTING,' and 'PRIVATE PROPERTY, NO ACCESS'.

'It's not exactly neighbourly,' I told him. 'All this would put people off buying here.'

'Nothing for sale here.'

'No gunfire today?'

He laughed. 'Only for strangers.'

'Who runs this place?'

'Intelligence.'

He took the bend fast and had no fear, and as a reward arrived at the hill I thought I remembered. Engine still running, he got a key from the glove compartment and unlocked a primitive electric gate. I couldn't see the hamlet.

'It's right at the top. You can't see it from the road.'

I must have approached in the past from another angle behind the chapel.

We drove up the deceptively steep hill and to one side I could see the mountains, the sweep of land, the abandoned monastery where Mario and Holland had, by their music, called up whirling dust. He curved around the last quarter mile and there were the buildings, sweet in the morning light. I couldn't see the school. Was this really the place? The public phone was gone. The house, its shutters closed, looked uninhibited. The chapel, at right angles to one side, facing the other buildings, looked chirpy in the first sunlight. The graveyard was sparse and the fountain dripping as though recently used. The air soft with a scented breeze, the light the colour of honey, made everything gentle, and after a while, optimistic. Far below, the sea and a stretch of uninhibited coast. The place was pure and innocent like the first spring morning ever, that renewed the feelings I used to have of excitement, adventure, the way it felt on the travels with Beryl. At the back, I could see a cowshed, a truck. 'There's no one here,' I told him.

'It's not meant for people,' he said. Then he took hold of me, hugged me close. 'Too much fear. There is nothing to fear here.' He gently massaged my back.

'But the person isn't here. You said earlier when I asked you questions, that the answers were better coming from the master.'

'Infinitely better,' he agreed.

'And you brought me here.'

'Exactly.'

And we stood apart, and the chapel bell tolled the hour.

'It is deserted.' And then the house door opened, and a man came towards us. He wore a fresh white shirt and bright white trousers. His clothes had been hand washed and dried outdoors in the wind and sun. First surprise, then the joy, as life lifted onto a higher scale as it would with him, all else forgotten. He came towards me bringing all the good things as he always had. I remembered people saying he was not of this world. He came from some other place touched by a life-joy we gravity-ridden ones could only acknowledge as it passed beyond us on its way.

224

So he was the master, was I really surprised? If I had known that, perhaps I'd have changed my approach to him over the years. That made me laugh. How did I address him now? Was his wife also here?

'So you followed the talisman they gave you?' he said. I stared at this man in the brilliant white shirt, standing out from everything around him, exuding light, specialness, power.

I said automatically. 'Do you believe in the Blue Apples?'

He pretended to consider the question, 'I prefer my apples red.'

We went into the house with its cool large kitchen and long oilskin-covered table. He poured us freshly made coffee and heated milk. Kim cut the fresh bread, put out the slab of butter, olives, figs. They spoke in Catalan, and it seemed they were arranging a special service in the chapel. They didn't seem to mind as I looked around the house. I remembered its generous staircase and tessellated floor, the balcony with its immense views, the mountains like curious neighbours in a line to the side of the courtyard the oriental woman had swept. And then, through an open door on a far wall, I saw one of the celestial maps, similar to those in the castle, and as I approached I could make out it was extraordinarily drawn with a power and richness I had not seen.

'It's coded.' And I realized Kim was behind me. Around the edges of the pictures, signs of unknown animals, lettering I did not recognize, and measurements I could not know. I asked what it was.

'Thuban,' said Kim.

José came up silently and closed the door, shutting off the picture. He said it was not good to look at it for long. I wondered if his wife was here, so I asked an easier question. Was the oriental woman here? 'I remember her sweeping the courtyard.'

'No,' said José, too fast.

I explained again about the previous visit and saw the eyes of the two men meet briefly.

'There is no such woman,' said José. 'The light here can do strange things.'

So I mentioned the statue of an oriental female in the Casa

Cundaro that disappeared between a night and a day. He did not reply.

We passed through the first-floor room with the terrace and I hated to leave. I belonged here. But José encouraged me to the staircase. One last look back at the room, as the sun hit the far wall and in that moment I saw one thing I needed. In the patch of arriving sunlight against the wall, her broom was resting. It was unlike any other, its bristles long and generous. José took my arm and I still stared at the wall. 'They don't make brooms like that anymore.'

We sat by the fountain and I said I needed to ask questions, and José gave me a few moments of serious consideration. In return, I looked at him, right through the past to the moment of crossing the clanking bridge, when I first arrived in Girona. 'We owe it to each other,' I said.

He suggested we look at the chapel which I'd last seen many years ago and couldn't remember. He'd got the key and we were inside a place that held an atmosphere I had never encountered. It was as though a large part of this atmosphere was out of reach of my senses, and discernment. What was there was too little and shrinking by the moment, and my nerve endings crawled after it, and then I realized I had encountered it before. It had something of the vacuum of occasional episodes in my hotel room. It smelt of a mustiness I could not locate and had silences and stillnesses beyond what I'd known. I supposed a child could feel like this, coming into this world.

But there was nothing here in this chapel which resonated with human life. I looked longingly at the blaze of light waiting at the open door, and hoped I could leave. I understood Kim to say, 'She doesn't recognize this.'

The altar, a simple stone slab, surrounded by seven dishes of oil, a flame burning in each. At the back, a line of enormously tall, white candles almost to the ceiling, with flames that dropped down the sides like tears.

'Just breathe,' said Kim, comforting me again. 'You will get used to it.' Dominating everything, the vast mural showing a line of Beings wearing long garments with purple borders and hoods, entering this chapel. The next section showed them present in this interior, and the last section when they left, without the hoods or ritual raiment. They became weightless and lifted up off into the sky. The more I absorbed the picture, the less aware I was of the chapel's atmosphere. The Beings travelled across a sky which became adorned with silver lights, joyous, sublime.

'They came from a divinity,' said Kim. 'A miracle happened here.'

José did not elaborate on the miracle, but pointed to the stone floor. 'Look at this, well. This is not found often.'

Because of his elevated position, I could no longer speak to him as I had. I said instead, 'Why didn't you tell me?' It covered everything. Did she, the wife, know? My thoughts were far from custodial.

The floor was designed for a connection to be created with another planet, Kim told me. A direct shaft between here and there, like a stairwell. The floor looked simple enough, patterned old stone – uniform. 'It's a planetarium. It all travels from here to there. We had to lift our energies to reach them and they, lower theirs to contact us.'

'Do we think as they do?' I asked.

'They can make a message clear in dreams. You could receive information while in a dream state.'

I asked about the miracle. José pointed at the painting. 'That tells you everything. It is coded. Count the figures waiting outside, and then those inside. The key is in the lock. It turns and you will see where life was transformed.'

Was this going to be the number we must not say?

'So the Beings going into this church and the ones that are already inside are the lock and key?' I asked. 'What about the ones outside?'

'They are now free.'

'But first you do the journey around the circles to this point,' said Kim kindly. 'To witness this transformation means you have completed the journey of initiation.'

The light in the doorway was a massive blast of brightness more than anything I had seen. 'Have I reached this point?'

Kim indicated we sit outside. As I left, I managed to see goblets in shapes I did not recognize.

'Here you can only see in part,' said Kim. 'You will never see this interior complete. It isn't arriving from our consciousness. We have years of development to free from the material plane before this interpretation can take place.'

I didn't have years. I noticed the master was not overly encouraging. Did he want me in this society? How would he explain it? After all, he may be a master, but he still had a wife to deal with.

I picked up a small object before leaving the chapel. It was deceptively heavy, and as I put it down quickly, Kim moved it to its rightful place. 'Everything has to be exact according to the measurements of the interior,' he said.

I asked who had designed it.

'Not us.' By the fountain in the shade, José said immediately, my being a part of its evolution was not his wish. I was a free spirit, a waif, a traveller taking the roads as they came. This position would be demanding, holding me in one place as it had him over the years. How many times had I heard he could not leave Girona? I wouldn't have argued as I usually did on account of his exalted role. He said I should go off and travel as always, and write my book.

I felt there was a touch of recrimination in that suggestion. Maybe he hadn't taken my journeys to and fro over the years as lightly as I had thought. I had to grab at some kind of acceptance. Rejection from him never did any good, so I said other people didn't necessarily see it as he did, but as he was the master I would try now — I wasn't sure what I would try.

'But I am not the master,' said José, 'I am the gardener.'

We circled down into the crypt and felt our way along an unlit passage. He led us into a cool stone room with facing ledges, like those in the Hapsburg castle vault. Here the atmosphere was light, and I had no expectation of troubled happenings to come, which in this situation could have crossed my mind. I had no sense of unwelcome consequences and suddenly realized I hadn't mentioned Gyp, but he didn't somehow belong to this place and his name alone could kill off what could be coming next. I did wonder if the master was the oriental lady. I hoped, whoever it was, it came from this world. A high stained-glass window let in a flutter of confetti light. I sat facing Kim on the stone ledge.

José asked me to listen well to what he was about to say.

'Here you dwelleth in the secret place of the most High. Apart from the world as you know it. From here you are given strength to face the world. Material things cannot intrude upon this secret place. They cannot ever find it because it is outside the realm of the material.'

I had to hold myself upright. I was worn out.

'The Highest Beings are here close to us. We ask for guidance to trust in the spiritual forms we cannot see.' He took my hand. 'Can you believe in the Unseen?'

This needed a reply and I said I could.

He took me swiftly into a chamber lit by spears of sunlight. A window at the end was open and it felt more like a conservatory than a place of ritual. Plants and flowers flourishing outside pressed against the window. I could smell earth and herbs. It reminded me of the place in France where my Grid numbers had been changed. Stones around the walls held lamps of all shapes and age. I thought I recognized from a long-ago visit, a flat horizontal structure like a measurement ruler, with circular indentations for oil which, when lit, provided light. It was said to be at least 2000 years old.

The statue of the oriental woman holding the crescent moon was now positioned in one corner, and I did wonder who brought it back from the Casa Cundaro or if it was ever there, and I had mistaken shadow for slanted eyes. Opposite, a ceramic figure of a modern girl with laughing eyes and white wings held a finger to her lips, asking for silence. José said she was showing me I must keep the secret. I was invited to sit on a low platform, and finally I looked in front of me at the long elegant dark-blue Stone Cradle. Fruit dish? Today, it was more like a slim, elegant boat. A faint smell of some unknown herb, the distant sound of bells, at one point I thought I heard voices of the circle children. José touched the Cradle so it rocked gently. He said quite simply, 'Ask your questions.'

Who would answer? Did the Cradle have a voice?

Kim smiled at me, encouraging, and again I thought I could hear the voices of the children.

'Who answers?' I said.

'Ask the questions in thought,' José said softly. 'And the answers will be given to you this day or later.' He glanced briefly at Kim, then lowered his head in respect and I was taken back out of there to sit by the fountain. Kim sprinkled water on my wrists, dabbed my forehead. Now I had loads of questions. José stayed inside the chapel.

'The Cradle is one of the oldest stones on the planet,' said Kim. 'It is a meteorite and arrived here, it seems, in that perfect shape. It exists in a vast cone of space with many dimensions, more than we have. If it is out of the three we inhabit — say it is moved between eight and nine dimensions — we can't see it and it becomes invisible. Dali said it exists on 23 different dimensions of time and space.'

'So it can become invisible?'

'Yes. We can't see it. So, although it is still there, for us it is invisible.'

'What was the miracle that brought transformation?'

'The arrival of the Child of Light.' And he added a year into the number Lewis Doyle had found so important, 5351. 'It brought evolvement, healing, a progression from the physical to the etheric. It brought power for this planet to progress.'

I asked why the Cradle was held in this secret place.

'Because human beings would misuse the powers and eventually destroy it and then themselves.'

Finally I asked him what was the purpose of the Child of Light.

'To open up your consciousness to the Will of the divine. It can show us the path. It can allow us to know the future. Through rituals, we can heal that past.'

Through the shutters, I could see into the kitchen as José prepared food, and I was sure the oriental woman was there.

'Do the locals know about this?' I asked.

'There are no locals as such, anymore. The land is owned in the society's name. 200 years ago the people around would come and sit on the hill. When they knew they were dying, some would come to lie in the Cradle. They put their sick children there to be made well.'

He told me the Cradle was now used for rituals. Initiates seated around it could reach into the past and, on occasion, bring back the time of the Child of Light.

'What is the Cradle?'

'The Cradle forms an interface between life and death. It also connects to the dream world. It is a Portal to other dimensions. It asks us to have faith in a non-established, non-material way of life. It holds the souls of those yet to be born.'

I asked him what it was made of.

'It's a meteorite. Rock iron and another element. Before it crashed through the meteorite belt it would have been as large as a double-decker bus. It is one of the oldest stones on the planet. It is in the care of other intelligences not of this earth.'

So I asked the purpose.

'When the Being left from here, the light remained. It moves around the planet in trails and traces, ever decreasing. It is our job to locate these traces and expand them and use them to lift the planet, its spirit.' He lowered his voice. 'So follow the traces and use them.'

After lunch which was made from the food of the land and the wine from Kim's vineyard, we walked to the other larger fountain with steps leading to the source, and seats around to take the waters. I understood José spent much of his time working on the grounds. I asked when the hamlet was built.

'The chapel third century. But a building was there before. The house 200 years. The school unknown. It was always there but constantly restored. From the beginning of known time.'

'Who built the place?'

'Not us,' said José. 'It is understood a cluster of Beings from a planet. Human-built, it would never have survived the winds.'

'What do they do, these Beings?'

José laughed. 'Their best.'

I asked what they looked like.

'I imagine like us,' Kim said. 'I am told one would recognize another.'

I asked who protected the place when José wasn't there.

'I don't protect it. It's protected by elementals, spirits and energies from other times.'

'Are they friendly Beings?'

'They chose to come here. This is theirs.' And he indicated a wide circle. 'It is understood they don't much like human beings. We are animal, gravity-bound, greedy, not spirit. We are hungry ghosts. We come here to see what we can take and grab as our own.'

'The power travels around the planet, spreading its light. Let's use it. Let's transform it for good while we can,' said Kim.

'Have you seen a Being from another existence?'

'I have not,' said Kim.

'But these Beings run this place and the society?'

He chose to look at José.

'Apparently that has been understood for many years,' said José.

'I remember when everything was open here. Yet now, it's electronic fences, locks, danger signs, the sound of gunfire. Who has asked for that?'

'Of course,' said José quickly, 'because people come here and take everything or destroy it. The time you remember, people did not even lock their doors.'

I still hadn't mentioned Gyp. That world did not belong up here. The very sound of his name — the chapel door slams shut. I wanted to protect this beautiful hour. The nearest we got to Gyp was Doyle.

232

'They stopped the American,' said José.

'They? You mean Doctor Arnau killed him?'

'No, he's just a worker. Doyle got too close. The Cradle is guarded by elementals, but also from afar. Just remember the landscape is the secret. I notice you didn't bring Gyp and you don't mention him.'

'That's right.' I looked away. Had he been killed? Did these men know?

José reminded me of the key he gave me in this place, many years ago. 'So you would begin the journey. It came from the Cradle decoration, one of the oldest pieces of lapis in the world. It allows the wearer to approach transformation. It certainly seemed to transform itself into the distance in your case.' He laughed. 'It was yours for a while.' And then he placed in my palm a piece of soft Blue Stone and folded it into my hand. It felt kind.

José went into the house and I told Kim I had never been aware of, or seen activity from beyond this planet. I assumed this existence was to learn; we were allowed choice. This was the waiting room. The planet was not in the centre of any galaxy but way off in the suburbs. It brought to attention the hotel room and the agitated state of waiting and the unusual sense of urgency beyond my control, as though I would be ripped apart by childbirth. I had felt something of that just now in the chapel.

He said I had been caught between reflecting energies. 'You are a sensitive which is one reason why Doctor Arnau wants you. But you don't bother to close down or protect yourself. You are wide open. Of course the Cradle calls to you and you are drawn to this place. The Cradle site is finite. Time is running out and when it comes to an end who knows what that brings. Doctor Arnau needs you. The custodial role will be mainly rituals and guidance. But José sees you as that travelling free person.'

Again that day, I remembered Beryl and that time of the frontier and the thrill of the unknown. I had no fear then. That was who I was, essentially. Life had just got in the way.

For some time the three of us sat on the hill with no more need to talk, and the light changed, it became the Blue Hour. José took my hand. 'You seem happy here.'

I thought, I belong here.

'Believe in the Unseen,' he said.

Would it give the answer?

We watched the last of the magnificent sunset still flaming as it sank below the horizon, and behind us the sky darkening and Venus already there as though impatient to be close to what was hers, and the rim of the crescent moon claiming a place, and we agreed all was well on this one exquisite day.

I sat opposite Dr Arnau and thanked him for picking me up but it was all done for. I had chickened out. He tried to talk me around but I said the truth. I had just come here because of a love story, it was done.

'But you, my friend, you can't get away. Gyp understood that.'

Past tense? Passed? Had he?

'I won't do it. But I won't say anything.'

'Who are the society?' he said. 'Do you know?'

I did not. Apart from him. The oriental woman? 'I understand they don't come from here.'

'That's settled then.' He was satisfied.

I got up as far as the door.

'But there's one thing. Don't forget your granddaughter.'

The summer 2014 in London was too hot and I told the grand-children we should go to the sea to a new place. I gave them a map of Europe to choose somewhere and minutes later I could hear quarrelling and the boys went out to play football and had for-gotten all about the holiday. My granddaughter came in carrying the map.

'So you've found somewhere?' I said pleased.

'I know where I want to go.'

She opened the map on the table and unerringly put a finger on the place. 'Rebés.'

Entering the hidden chapel